D1449004

Presented to

_____

by

_____

On the Occasion of

_____

Date

_____

Romance
IN REAL LIFE

101 Tips and Inspiration for
Improving Your Marriage

ELLYN SANNA
WITH J. LEE STEWART

BARBOUR BOOKS
An Imprint of Barbour Publishing, Inc.

Cover art © PhotoDisc, Inc.

ISBN 1-58660-493-7

Published by Barbour Books, an imprint of Barbour Publishing, Inc.,
P.O. Box 719, Uhrichsville, Ohio 44683
www.barbourbooks.com

Member of the
Evangelical Christian
Publishers Association

Printed in the United States of America.

Romance
IN REAL LIFE

101 Tips and Inspiration for
Improving Your Marriage

This one is for Paul.
(Who else?)

CONTENTS

INTRODUCTION

The specific graces of marriage—
the ability to trust myself to another,
to forgive and be forgiven,
to communicate and confront effectively. . .
are indeed gifts of God.
Yet they include much personal effort. . . .
Marriage requires that I be able
to risk myself in close contact with another—
in love, in sex, in cooperation, in conflict.

EVELYN EATON WHITEHEAD
and JAMES D. WHITEHEAD

This book is a part of a series designed for women who juggle their lives. In other words, as wives and mothers, all of us women have one hundred and one "balls" we try to keep up in the air on any given day. We are housekeepers and lovers, cooks and counselors, chauffeurs and nurses, veterinarians and launderers, seamstresses and teachers—and we perform all these roles while at the same time we struggle to meet our outside obligations as wage earners, volunteers, daughters, and friends. It's no wonder if our juggling routines sometimes become frantic, desperate, even chaotic. Some days we're simply overwhelmed by all we have to do.

The "Juggling Our Lives" books are designed to help women cope with all their roles and responsibilities a little more smoothly—and this particular book focuses on the marriage "ball." In the midst of all we have to do, we do not want to lose sight of our husbands.

And yet, realistically, we simply don't have time to set all the other balls down and focus completely on our marriage. If we could, we might be able to toss this one ball smoothly up and down, up and down, with nary a drop or fumble—but the concrete facts of our lives simply won't allow us to do that. Too many other people are depending on us.

This book won't ask you to drop everything else and put your marriage at the center of your life. Instead, each piece of advice will simply offer you a small hint you can incorporate into your juggling routine, a juggling tip that will enrich and strengthen your marriage. Of course, at first you may have to make a conscious effort to practice these tips, but as you do so, gradually they will become habits. And the blessing of habits is that they can help us shape our lives with patterns of action that are loving and effective, patterns we don't have to reach and stretch for because they are already available to us.

These habitual patterns of action will help make our juggling routines more graceful. If you look at an actual juggler, one who juggles real balls instead of responsibilities, what she's doing—keeping all those balls in the air—may look to you like magic. Really, though, what you're seeing are habits that the juggler has built out of many hours of practice. The juggler's effort and discipline result in well-established habits, habits of gracefulness. We too can do the same with our lives.

In all the books in this series I recommend that you make God the center of your juggling routine. When He is the focus of our busy days, then all the many details of our lives are caught up into the rhythm of His grace—and we can rely on Him to catch the balls we sometimes can't help dropping. This book is designed to help you include the marriage "ball" in a juggling routine that focuses on God.

You'll find that the book's text is a song in two-part harmony: J. Lee Stewart, a licensed psychologist who has worked professionally with families and couples, created the 101 tips to improve your marriage, while I wrote my own response to each of his ideas. He also supplied extra informational material to supplement and expand some of his pointers.

Writing a book with a professional in this way was a new experience for me, and I found that my own marriage experience was challenged and strengthened as Lee and I worked together. It became very difficult for me to continue practicing a bad habit in my marriage when I couldn't help but hear one of Lee's marriage tips whispering a reminder at the back of my mind! Lee's successful track record, both as a well-educated professional and as a long and happily married man, gave me added confidence in his ideas.

My prayer is that your marriage will also be empowered as you incorporate Lee's advice into your juggling routine.

Marriage is not so unlike juggling. . . .
To do it well requires
a variety of skills and abilities.
And sustained discipline is required
if one is to learn to live
this complex and enduring relationship gracefully.

EVELYN EATON WHITEHEAD
and JAMES D. WHITEHEAD

CO-AUTHOR'S FOREWORD

When Ellyn Sanna asked me to collaborate on a small book of ideas for improving marriages, I was both pleased to be asked and too quick to think my part of the project would be fairly easy. (Writing is hard!)

I found that every book has many authors. For my part, this book is the product of many things: a fairly long and continuing education, opportunities to learn from families with whom I've worked professionally, one hundred and one sermons on marriage, the much-to-be-emulated and long-lasting unions of my own parents and in-laws, and many years married to one person. Faith Stewart, psychologist and school administrator, my partner for thirty years, made many helpful suggestions and comments for this book—and she's taught me most of what's worth knowing about marriage. She also undoubtedly (and thoughtfully) kept her own counsel when she determined it was kinder to do so. She is truly the Wise One in my life.

My part in this book is offered in her honor—and in loving memory of Jackson and Betty Stewart, my first teachers about life in general and marriage in particular.

Also, I want to say a word of thanks to Ellyn Sanna. When I saw the finished product this book became, I was more than ever in awe of her gifts as a writer, the depth of her Christian insight and faith, and how much she has learned about marriage in such a short time. (Seventeen years is just the beginning, Ellyn!) Thanks for thinking of me when you conceived this project.

J. LEE STEWART

CHAPTER ONE

*Taking Care of
the Two of You*

Love sends a strong, clear message.
It says, "I'm here for you,
you are a major priority,
you can count on me.
Your happiness and well-being
are just as important to me as my own."

EVELYN AND PAUL MOSCHETTA

1

Make your marriage your number-one priority after your relationship with God.

As women juggling our busy lives, it's all too easy to let our marriages fall into the background. We would never say our marriages weren't important—and yet we act as though they're not.

Almost any time management book will tell you that one of the first steps toward using your time more effectively is to write down your priorities—and then use your time in a way that reflects those priorities. That may mean we have to say no to other responsibilities and pleasures. But if our relationships with our husbands are a priority in our lives, then we will not consider time spent enjoying them to be time wasted. Instead, we will make certain we allow space in each day for our marriage—even if that means there's no time left over to clean the house or talk on the phone with a friend or catch up on the laundry.

ROMANCE IN REAL LIFE

The plain fact is that most of us
do not take marriage seriously.
We get so caught up in all the other demands that
our marriage and the quality of our togetherness
fall to the bottom of our "to do" list.

EVELYN AND PAUL MOSCHETTA

? ?
. .

*If marriage is a vocation that begins
in a resounding "yes,"
it matures in many "no's."
To have quality time for my partner
and our family
I find I have to say "no"
to many outside demands and requests.*

EVELYN EATON WHITEHEAD
AND JAMES D. WHITEHEAD

2
Make a choice to be married every day.

Being married isn't a decision you can make once and then be done with it. The wedding ceremony does not magically transform us into "married people." Instead, being married is a lifetime process, one that we must commit ourselves to again and again. We must choose to be married over and over.

In terms of the juggling metaphor, the marriage "ball" is not one we can allow to bounce off into the corner, where it can lie forgotten and dusty for days. Each and every day (and night), we make the choice to keep this ball up in the air.

*The marriage ceremony
isn't like graduation;
rather it's similar to the first day
of kindergarten!
It's not the culmination,
but the beginning.*

SUSAN ALEXANDER YATES

ROMANCE IN REAL LIFE

Marriage has no automatic pilot. You can't flick
a switch and lean back and forget about it.
You have to stay at the controls, making
adjustments, making it fly. Every day you have
to decide to love your mate. Every day.

KEVIN LEMAN

This is a maturing love of choice.
In the light of this deepening awareness of who you
are and who I really am,
I choose anew to love you.
I reaffirm the commitment to do
"whatever is necessary" so that this relationship
in which we hold each other may live and grow.

EVELYN EATON WHITEHEAD
AND JAMES D. WHITEHEAD

3

*Catch your partner being good,
and tell him about it.*

*(Watch for sarcasm in your voice,
as praise can be tricky; it may sound backhanded,
especially if you're uncomfortable or insincere.
Practice with a friend or in front of a mirror
if you know you'll have trouble.)*

Sometimes we get so accustomed to interacting with our husbands in a certain way that we're embarrassed to try a new way. "We just don't do that," you may say in response to Lee's advice.

But that doesn't mean we can't try new ways of relating to our husbands, ways that will strengthen our marriages rather than weaken them. Instead of letting our husbands know all the things they do wrong, imagine how they'd feel if we let them know all the things they do right. As mothers, most of us try to apply this principle to our interactions with our children, but praise is just as effective with adults as it is with children.

The behaviors to which we pay attention—even when our attention is negative—are usually the ones that will be repeated. So encourage your husband to repeat the behaviors you love, instead of the ones you dislike. No matter how hard it may seem at first, praise changes the quality of a relationship. And the more you practice expressing your appreciation to your husband, the easier it becomes.

Love must be sincere. . .
cling to what is good.

ROMANS 12:9

⸮ ⸮

Whatever is true, whatever is noble,
whatever is right,
whatever is pure, whatever is lovely,
whatever is admirable—
if anything is excellent or praiseworthy—
think about such things.

PHILLIPIANS 4:8

4

*Always greet each other with
your full attention.*

Recently, I realized I had developed a bad habit. When my husband came home from work, I would often be busy with some occupation of my own. Concentrating on finishing the job at hand, I would barely look up as I give him an absentminded hello. I didn't realize the unspoken message my preoccupation was conveying, until one day the shoe was on the other foot: I walked in the door after a late meeting, anticipating the warmth of my husband's arms—but instead, I had to hunt him down, and when I finally found him, his greeting was lukewarm to say the least. Hurt, I found myself whining, "Don't you care that I'm home? Aren't I important to you?"

Since then, we've been more careful about our greetings. When we're reunited at the end of the workday, we stop whatever else we're doing and welcome each other home—and if one of us forgets this small ceremony, the other prompts the forgetful one with a word of reminder. These small reunions may seem unimportant—but they are opportunities to say, "I appreciate you. I'm glad we share our lives. You're important to me."

ROMANCE IN REAL LIFE

A simple greeting can become a genuine
celebration that says. . . ,
"You're special."

SUSAN ALEXANDER YATES

⟨ ⟩

Greet one another
with a holy kiss.

1 CORINTHIANS 16:20

5
Say "I love you" often.

This seems so simple—but I know from experience how important it is. The more often we say the words, the more secure my husband and I feel with each other. And the more often I express my love, the more loving I feel as well. Instead of a "vicious circle," this is productive circle that goes round and round, the words strengthening the feeling that inspires the words, and on and on.

What's more, I don't have to wait for my husband to be the first to start this loving cycle. I find that the more I express my love to him, the more apt he is to respond with his own expressions of love. I guess that's just another one of those creative cycles we sometimes miss when we spend our time trapped in "vicious circles" instead.

> *They do not love that*
> *do not show their love.*

WILLIAM SHAKESPEARE

ROMANCE IN REAL LIFE

*What good is my love if it stays in
my heart,
hidden from the world and from
[my partner]?
Love can be an action as simple as
doing the vacuuming. . .
making dinner. . .an unexpected
hug.
Love can even be as simple as giving
[my partner]
more attention than I give to the TV.*

HENRY JAMES BORYS

♡ Saying "I Love You" Without Saying a Word.

You don't always have to use words to express your love. In fact some people feel most loved when the message is conveyed to them in some concrete, tangible way. Here's one example:

Hide a fancy chocolate (or its functional equivalent—something small your husband will be pleased to find) in an unexpected place. . .his pillow, the pocket of his suit jacket, or in his suitcase if he has to be away from home.

6.
Understand the language your husband uses to express love.

Each of us expresses love in different ways. For some of us (like me) verbal expressions are most important—but others depend more on acts of kindness, gifts, companionship, or some other more tangible demonstration of affection.

Unfortunately, if words are the only language you understand, you may miss the very real expressions of love your husband is sending your way. For instance, some weeks I feel particularly insecure because I haven't heard my husband say, "I love you"— and meanwhile, he's wondering what my problem is, since he's taken my car to the service station, vacuumed the living room, and brought me a bowl of ice cream after supper without me even asking. "You never say you love me," I whine. And he just throws up his hands in exasperation, thinking (I suspect), *I obviously love you.*

Learning a foreign language can be difficult— but doing so tends to promote unity. The same principle applies to marriage.

And who knows? Your husband may feel a bit more secure if you try expressing your love to him in the language he understands best.

If you were to move to France,
it would take a while for you
to pick up the language.
The same is true of love
languages.
Don't demand too much too
soon.
They take a while to speak
fluently.

KEVIN LEMAN

7.
*If you have to be away overnight,
call home and call often.*

As I write these words, my husband happens to be more than six hundred miles away from me. This is the second time we've been apart in the past month, and I'm missing him. When we're not together, I realize all over again how glad I am that I'm married. I wouldn't want to be a single person again—and I still choose my husband as the person I most want to be with in all the world.

But occasional separations are often unavoidable. When circumstances demand that my husband and I go different directions temporarily, it's all too easy to lose touch with one another. Our daily routines no longer bind us together, and the gradual accumulation of our separate days' events pile up between us.

That's why it's important for us to talk on the phone as often as we can. My husband's not a real verbal guy, and I suspect he finds our evening telephone time together as unsatisfactory as I do. Communicating the events of our days just isn't the same as feeling his arms around me, or curling up in bed together. But we still call each other every night. We need to reach across the miles and affirm: *I still love you. No matter how far apart we are, in my heart I am still married to you.*

We don't want the physical distance to turn into emotional distance.

> *May the Lord keep watch*
> *between you and me*
> *when we are away from each other.*

GENESIS 31:49

⁀ ⁀

Like cold water to weary soul
is good news from a distant land.

PROVERBS 25:25

8.

Practice making requests rather than demands.

"You're acting like a selfish princess," we used to say to our daughter when she was younger. But I have to admit I have a selfish princess who lives inside me as well. She's the one who wants the best and the biggest served up to her by a humble and loving slave. All too often, I expect that slave to be my husband. And when he doesn't always cooperate, I'm as frustrated and angry as any four year old.

When my requests turn into demands, however, I'm failing to respect my husband's personhood. He is not my slave; he was not put on earth for my sole convenience. Slavery sees another human being as a mere object, but true love honors that person.

Demands are put-downs, implying,
"I'm important and you're not. . . ."
On the other hand,
a humble request gives the other
person a choice.

KEVIN LEMAN

For even I, the Son of Man,
came here not to be served
but to serve others. . . .

JESUS OF NAZARETH
(MATTHEW 20:28 NLT)

9.

*As a general rule you shouldn't say no
to your partner when you can easily say yes.*

**(This doesn't mean you should tolerate an abusive
partner. I'm talking about the freely given courtesies
two people who love each other enjoy giving.)**

Lee's point here makes me think, I have to admit. Do I have a "yes" policy with my husband—or do I say yes only when it's convenient for me?

As I think about it, though, I realize my husband seldom asks me for anything I find unreasonable or too demanding. Sometimes he asks me to scratch his back or get him a drink when he's working. Once in a while one or the other of us gets an ice cream craving after the kids are in bed, and whoever is craving the treat persuades the other one to drive to the grocery store. Most of the time he doesn't exactly ask, he just hints—like when I haven't made his favorite lentil soup in a while. By the same token, sometimes when we're both in bed, I'll start complaining about how thirsty I am; he'll groan, but he gets up to get me a glass of water.

But those are easy requests. As I think about Lee's advice a bit more, I recall an event that happened a couple of weeks ago. Our family car needed repairs, and my husband and I had agreed to meet at a certain time at the service station. We would leave the family car, and then I'd take the car he usually drives and drop him off back at work, leaving me free to run the many errands I needed to do that day. The schedule I had planned for myself was a tight one, so I was irritated when I arrived at the service station and found that my husband wasn't there. When I called him on the cell phone, in a brusque voice he asked me to wait for him a bit longer. As an hour ticked away, I became impatient; by the time he arrived, I was fuming.

"I'm sorry I made you wait," he said.

I took a deep breath. I knew he was expecting my anger; I'm not known for my patience when I feel he infringes on my time like that. To my surprise, I heard myself say, "That's all right. I assume you wouldn't have done it if you hadn't had a good reason."

He looked surprised and then relieved. As it turned out, my trust was not misplaced. He had had a safety crisis at work, something he couldn't discuss over the phone. My saying yes this time, when it wasn't easy, brought us closer.

Sometimes it is difficult to say yes to our husbands. It means taking a small leap of faith. But it's one more way we can demonstrate not only our love but our trust.

ROMANCE IN REAL LIFE

Capitulation means giving in,
    giving a gift to your partner by giving in
    to what he or she asks and needs of you.

EVELYN AND PAUL MOSCHETTA

 ⸮ ⸮

*What do we live for,
if not to make life less difficult for each other?*

GEORGE ELIOT

If You're Uncomfortable with Your Husband's Requests

In a mature relationship where both partners trust the other, saying yes to each other's requests is simply one way to demonstrate your love. But if you're starting to feel uneasy saying yes, you should ask yourself why. There are a couple of possibilities.

• Is your husband asking you to grow in ways you're uncertain about? (For instance, if your husband asks you to participate in a sport you lack confidence playing. . .or if he asks you to pray out loud with him. . .or if he asks you to attend a social function where you know you'll feel shy.) In these cases, it's your own fear and lack of self-confidence that may be holding you back; taking the leap of faith that saying yes demands may bring the two of you closer and help you grow as a person.

- But on the other hand, sometimes there is a fine line between being a loving wife and being a doormat. If you're starting to feel the requests go only one way (that he never says yes to you), or that his requests are more like demands, maybe it's time for a reality check. If necessary talk to someone objective (probably not your mother or your best friend who always takes your side), someone who can help you see your marriage relationship more clearly. If you feel your trust is being abused, talk to your husband about your feelings. If necessary talk with a professional counselor. And never feel you have to say yes to anything that is dangerous or demeaning to you as a person.

ROMANCE IN REAL LIFE

10.
Practice bringing your husband an unexpected gift that couldn't be for anybody else, especially for you.

*(A CD by your husband's favorite artist—
not yours—a book you wouldn't read
in a million years, the bitter chocolate
he loves but you can't abide.)*

Giving a gift is just saying "I love you" with a tangible object rather than with words. For some people the language of gifts is more important than it is for others, but almost all of us—including husbands—still have a child inside who remembers the magic of birthdays and Christmas mornings.

Gifts are like God's grace: We can do nothing to earn them; they come to us simply as free expressions of love. By the same token, we do not owe our husbands gifts—but when we give our husbands presents, we weave yet another strand into the growing fabric of our love.

Gifts are visual symbols of love.

GARY CHAPMAN

*A marriage can be improved
in many ways,
but I cannot think of one
that does not have
something to do with giving.*

HENRY JAMES BORYS

ROMANCE IN REAL LIFE

11.
*Schedule a date night with your husband
as often as you can. Make a date
with each other at least once a month.*

*(I can already hear a litany of excuses—
but don't let those excuses keep you from
enjoying a social evening with your best friend.)*

The most common reasons why we don't have more "date nights" with our husbands usually have to do with money and children. I personally have found that finding a satisfactory baby-sitter sometimes takes more time and energy than I have on hand. And if I do manage to find one, the cost of paying for her time on top of dinner and a movie seems like just too much. But if my relationship with my husband is a priority, then surely finding ways to spend time alone with him should be worth whatever it takes.

And when the demands of our families and our budgets just don't allow for an evening out, nothing says a "date" can't happen at home as well. No matter how busy our lives, most of us could schedule one night a week when as husbands and wives we simply concentrate on enjoying each other's presence, the way we used to when we were dating. To make the evening special, all we need to do is use our imaginations.

ROMANCE IN REAL LIFE

Here are some suggestions:

- Feed the children something simple and put them to bed; then enjoy a special grown-up meal just for the two of you.
- Light candles.
- Play soft music.
- Rent a video you'll both enjoy.
- Play cards or a board game together.
- Sit on the porch or by the fire and hold hands.

The pleasure of love is in loving.

FRANCOIS, DUC DE LA ROUCHEFOUCAULD

12.

Take turns doing the dirty work.

*(With all due respect for the joys of parenthood,
the "dirty work" often includes
a variety of child-care tasks.
No matter how much we love our kids,
they are born selfish and demanding;
coping with their legitimate needs—
their crankiness and squabbles,
their frequent illnesses, their school problems,
etcetera—is a formula for parental depression if one
person does the majority of the high-tension work.)*

I suspect that most wives feel they do more than their share of the "dirty work." If you feel like this, you need to make a time to talk it over with your husband. (Don't bring up the topic when you're in the midst of a fight, and try to find an occasion when neither of you are apt to become defensive or irritated.)

You may, however, be surprised to find that he feels he's doing his own share of tiresome tasks. (For instance, my husband tells me he gets tired of always being the person responsible for automobile maintenance.) Maybe you could trade off on some jobs. Offering to do some of "his" work will make him feel loved—and he'll be more receptive to doing his share of "your" work.

Whenever two people live together, whether they're husband and wife or not, the household work needs to be divvied up fairly. For instance, my husband and I have this deal: Whoever cooks supper doesn't have to clean up afterward. And I remember we used to take turns with dirty diapers. What works for one couple may not work for another; each married couple will have to find the division of labor that works best for them.

Honor one another above yourselves.

ROMANS 12:10

$\}\}$

Marriage is not just spiritual communion
  and passionate embraces; marriage is also
  three meals a day, sharing the workload
  and remembering to carry out the trash.

JOYCE BROTHERS

13.

Write your partner an unexpected love letter.

*(Better yet, make a habit of writing
your partner love letters.)*

I have to admit my husband's not the sort of guy who makes a habit of writing me long, romantic letters. But on my birthdays (and sometimes on other occasions), he writes me a note in a card. Since I'm far more comfortable expressing myself in writing than he is, his collection of love notes (and ten-page letters) is a bit more extensive than mine—but I've saved each and every card he's given me. I plan to keep them until I die.

Something about putting your love in writing makes it seem more tangible. It's a permanent record, something to warm your mate both now and in the future. What's more, often you can reveal yourself more deeply in writing than you might in person. Even my practical, no-frills husband writes me endearments he would never speak out loud.

Love spends all, and still hath store.

PHILIP JAMES BAILEY

♡ *Get* a copy of Ronald Reagan's collected love letters to Nancy to see how a good love letter is written. They may seem a little dated, but in my opinion they are one of Ronald Reagan's important legacies.

14.

Don't mistake intimacy for an exaggerated freedom to engage in annoying habits.

(Let's not misuse the unconditional positive regard we seek from our spouses.)

In Lee's first draft, he mentioned belching and other gross behaviors here. "Oh, come on," I said, "how many wives need this reminder?" But then I realized almost all of us have one or two annoying habits. For instance, when I'm bored, I tend to pick at my fingernails—and it really bugs my husband.

I used to have the attitude that Lee is advising against here; I felt that if my husband loved me, he should tolerate my little habits. I've begun to look at this the other way around now, however: If I love my husband, why should I make him endure something that irritates him?

Extraordinary closeness is bought at a cost, and the cost is nothing more nor less than one's own self.

No one has ever been married without being shocked at the enormity of this price and the monstrous inconvenience of this thing called intimacy which suddenly invades all life.

MIKE MASON

15.

Look for ways to be nice to your husband.

Marriage is an occasion to practice the gospel day in and day out. Our culture usually looks at things differently; most people spend their lives looking for ways that others can be of use to them. We may have entered marriage with that same attitude, expecting our husbands to do nice things for us, rather than seeking opportunities to demonstrate our love to them.

But if we want our marriages to grow and flourish, we will follow the pattern for love that Christ lived: We will look for opportunities to lay down our lives, to put our love into practice. In the context of our daily lives, this seldom means we literally give up our lives for the men we love. More likely, it means we pick up their dry cleaning—or take out the trash for them when they're running late.

*A growing relationship means
turning romantic love inside out—
from love that takes to love that gives.*

HENRY JAMES BORYS

ROMANCE IN REAL LIFE

It is not true that love makes all things easy;
it makes us choose what is difficult.

GEORGE ELIOT

*Here are some ideas for showing your love
through unexpected favors:*

- Clean the ice off his car in the morning.
- Do one of his chores for him (like taking out the garbage or having the car's oil changed).
- Fill his gas tank.
- Iron his shirts.
- Make his favorite meal or dessert.
- Bring him the paper.
- Make him breakfast in bed.
- Make him breakfast to go when he's running late for work.

16.

Make time to talk with your partner every day.

*(If you don't have time during a given day,
make an appointment to speak,
however briefly, on the phone.)*

We all have busy lives; most of us are juggling a multitude of different "balls" on any given day. In the midst of household responsibilities, jobs, children, and the swarm of other people in our lives who want something from us, we often lose track of our husbands. Entire days go by when my husband and I communicate little more than our good-bye kiss in the morning, our hello kiss at the end of the workday, and our good-night kiss before we go to sleep.

Three kisses a day, though, just aren't enough to sustain the most important relationship in my life. Even if we're not experiencing any real conflict, little by little the distance between us grows. Sooner or later, we realize that our sense of unity has become strained and starved.

As women who juggle our lives, we may not have time every day when we can sit down with our husbands, gaze into their eyes, and bare our souls— but we can talk to them while we share household chores, during car rides (no matter how short), and in bed before we fall asleep. And sometimes, as Lee suggests, we may even need to grab a few minutes in the midst of our days and call our husbands on the phone.

> *Love is possible only if*
> *two persons communicate*
> *with each other from the center*
> *of their existence.*

ERIC FROMM

17.
*Spend time celebrating important events
in your relationship.*

*(Don't limit yourself to the obvious,
like your wedding anniversary—
but don't let that slide either).*

According to the old stereotypes, husbands are the ones who forget these important celebrations. Unfortunately, as we wives juggle more and more responsibilities, we too may become forgetful. Many of my friends have complained recently they just don't have time this year for celebrating anniversaries. . .or Valentine's Day. . .or Father's Day. I have to confess I've been guilty of this as well. Just keeping up with the family birthdays seems like all I can manage.

But if my marriage is the most important human relationship in my life, then I need to affirm and strengthen my love for my husband by rejoicing in it whenever I can. Celebrations don't need to be expensive or time-consuming; even the simplest traditions can celebrate our love. As the Bible says, in joy we find strength.

ROMANCE IN REAL LIFE

Go and enjoy choice food and sweet drinks. . . .
This day is sacred to our Lord.
Do not grieve, for the joy
of the LORD is your strength.

NEHEMIAH 8:10

≀ ≀

Celebration keeps us balanced in
a difficult world,
renews our perspective, and enables
us to recapture joy.

SUSAN ALEXANDER YATES

18.
*Find an activity you both enjoy doing—
and make time for it regularly.*

For some couples, this advice may be easy to follow—but others may find it more of a challenge. I love my husband dearly; he is truly my best friend; and there is no other person in the world with whom I enjoy being more. That said, I have to add we don't share a lot of interests. He's musical; I'm not. I love books; he doesn't. So when we relax together, a lot of the time he plays his guitar while I read. And we're both happy.

Mutually compatible activities are all well and good, but they don't bind us together the way a shared activity does. I admit that it takes far less effort to simply resign myself to the differences between my husband and me. But I don't want our lives to merely run parallel; I want them to be actively engaged with one another. Finding an activity we both enjoy knits us closer.

Quality time does not mean that we have to spend our together moments gazing into each other's eyes. It means that we are doing something together and that that we are giving our full attention to the other person.

GARY CHAPMAN

ROMANCE IN REAL LIFE

Lee's perspective:

My wife and I enjoy reading aloud to one another. We look for content that is mutually pleasurable; in our case, that usually means mysteries and suspense novels. Taking turns reading is the ideal, but we also accept exchanges for other courtesies instead (like back rubs or cleaning the kitchen).

Here are some activities you may enjoy as a couple:

- Gardening
- Playing cards or board games
- Remodeling projects
- Dancing
- People-watching
- Pillow fights
- Showering
- Cooking
- Tennis
- Walking
- Swimming
- Horseback riding
- Skiing
- Antiquing
- Refinishing projects
- Learning a language
- Playing with your children
- Shopping

19.

Spend money and / or effort making your bedroom a private retreat for the two of you.

I keep my living room picked up (most of the time)—but piles of stuff tend to accumulate in the bedroom that belongs to my husband and me. Along the same lines, I decorate my living room carefully, while the décor in our bedroom tends to be a haphazard affair. These habits, though, reflect and reinforce a skewed perspective: I want guests to be impressed by my living room more than I want to create a comfortable and attractive setting for the private moments I share only with my husband.

If my marriage is a priority, then creating a haven for that relationship is a necessity rather than an option. It's one way to take care of our marriages.

I will make a palace
fit for you and me. . . .

ROBERT LOUIS STEVENSON

ROMANCE IN REAL LIFE

20.
Schedule little honeymoons.

*(These should be far enough away from
home and work responsibilities
to provide time to relax and "recharge"
as a couple. If you have children,
this will be more complicated
but probably more critically needed.)*

The whole point of a honeymoon is to give a couple time to concentrate only on each other, away from the distractions and disruptions of daily life. We who have been married for a while probably need times like these even more than newlyweds do!

*Let us love one another,
for love comes from God.*

1 JOHN 4:7

21.

*Make it a practice to go to bed
at the same time as your husband.*

(At least several times a week.)

Going to bed at different times seems like such a little thing. After all, husbands and wives are two separate individuals with different schedules and physical cycles. For instance, sometimes I stay up late, pushing myself to meet a writing deadline, while my husband peacefully snores. Other times, he stays up to watch a late movie while I fall into bed exhausted as soon as the kids are asleep. Unfortunately, however, my husband and I are apt to fall into this pattern at the very times we most need moments of togetherness, during periods of our lives when we're so busy we have little time left over for each other.

Going to bed at the same time may be a little thing. But it's one of the small habits that will help us juggle our marriage "ball" more smoothly. Think about it: If you and your husband go to bed at the same time, you're more apt to talk for a few minutes or even laugh together before you fall asleep. You're more likely to snuggle close, enjoying the warmth and security of each other's presence. You might even find you make love more often.

*Love is the expansion
of two natures in such
a fashion that each
includes the other,
each is enriched
by the other.*

FELIX ADLER

ROMANCE IN REAL LIFE

22.
Take turns in conversation.

*(Allow at least 50 percent of the time
you spend talking with your husband for listening.)*

My husband's not a particularly verbal person. On the other hand, I am. So when we talk, I tend to rattle off ten sentences for every word he utters. (I don't think that's an exaggeration!) And then I complain he never talks to me.

Maybe he would if I just gave him the chance.

*Give all your attention,
all your energy to listening.
For this your ego must be out of the way.*

EVELYN AND PAUL MOSCHETTA

$$ \text{? ?} $$

Everyone should be quick to listen,
slow to speak and slow to become angry.

JAMES 1:19

If you want to be listened to,
you should put
in time listening.

MARGE PIERCY

23.

*Make your response to your partner's
shortcomings as different from the rest
of the world's as you possibly can.*

*(A best friend is the one who stands with you
against the world. Should our partners expect less?
Be that rare friend who stands with
your husband and his point of view, even when he's
been foolish, shortsighted, or dead wrong.)*

We all need to know that at least one person will always be on our side. My husband may not always approve of my actions—but I can always count on him to see my side and defend me against the rest of the world. When I'm embarrassed or feeling like I've messed up, I know I can run into his arms.

I hope he knows he can do the same.

*The atmosphere of our homes will either encourage or
discourage the building of strong marriage friendships.
Our homes should be, above all,
a place of acceptance—a place where
we don't have to worry about measuring up.
A place where we are loved simply because we belong.*

SUSAN ALEXANDER YATES

Psychologist Carl Rogers referred to "unconditional positive regard," when he wrote decades ago about the important components of a helping relationship. The ability to just care about your partner—and communicate your concern without a lot of judgmental stuff thrown in—is the essence, I think, of a healthy intimate relationship.

24.
*Sometimes you need to acknowledge
and accommodate each other's differences.*

*(Where is it written that marriage partners
have to do everything together?)*

My husband and I are two very different people. Sometimes these differences frustrate me. Occasionally, they hurt me. Often they intrigue me. Many times his strengths balance my weaknesses—and vice versa. Other times, he shows me that feelings can be expressed without saying a word, while I pull him out of his silences. And sometimes we need to simply go our separate ways temporarily.

As close as wives and husbands may be, as real as their unions are, ultimately we each stand alone in God's presence. One of the best gifts of love we can offer our husbands is to accept their differences with flexibility and tolerance.

*Constant togetherness is fine—
but only for Siamese twins.*

VICTORIA BILLINGS

ROMANCE IN REAL LIFE

Marriage seems to specialize, at times, in radically de-emphasizing the similarities between partners and wildly exaggerating the points of difference. . .so that a couple may be reduced to sheer amazement that they are together at all, and that they may know that what has brought them together and what keeps them together is something entirely outside of themselves, something not natural but supernatural, something which they themselves cannot control or produce at will.

MIKE MASON

?⁝?

Once the realization is accepted that
even between the closest human beings
infinite distances continue to exist,
a wonderful living side by side can grow
up, if they succeed in loving the distance
between them which makes it possible for
each to see
the other whole and against a wide sky.

RAINER MARIA RILKE

25.
*Do what you can to help your mate be active
and eat right.*

*(It's also okay to nudge a spouse who
avoids doctors to get the kind of
routine checkups and maintenance we all need,
especially as we get a little older.
The first and best thing you can do
is set a good example!)*

No one likes to feel nagged. But if we express ourselves carefully, gently, lovingly, then no matter how
reluctant our husbands may be, inside they will recognize our concern as a message of love.

Love detests what destroys the beloved.

REBECCA MANLEY PIPPERT

26.

Practice not whining,
and see if your partner will do the same.

We can choose how we want to respond to life's disappointments. When we make an effort to complain less, we usually find that the tenor of our conversations begins to change as well. Whining is contagious—and so is laughter.

As selfishness and complaint pervert
and cloud the mind,
so love with its joy clears
and sharpens the vision.

HELEN KELLER

ROMANCE IN REAL LIFE

27.
Don't compare your husband to others.

Sometimes it's easy to look at what someone else has and feel envious. I used to spend a lot of time wishing my husband were more like the spouse of a friend of mine. This man brought his wife flowers for no occasion whatsoever; he surprised her with candlelit dinners; he sent her romantic cards in the mail; and he even expressed his feelings fluently in sentences of more than three words each. My husband has never done any of those things, even when we were dating. Turned out, though, this particular man also had a problem with alcohol and fidelity.

The point is this: Each husband has his own unique strengths and weaknesses. (Just as each wife does.) We can learn from the marriages of others, but ultimately we have to live with our own husband and no one else. So appreciate and honor your husband's many gifts—and don't expect him to be anyone but who he is.

We are to learn from one another's marriages and to be encouraged by them, but at the same time, we must remember that every marriage is different.

SUSAN ALEXANDER YATES

*Every couple's journey
on the way of marriage
is uniquely their own.
There may be patterns
and principles
we can learn from each other,
but there are no pat formulas.*

HENRY JAMES BORYS

28.
Expect marriage to be hard work.

Romantic books and movies don't prepare us for marriage's reality. From the time we were children, we were raised on the words, "And they lived happily ever after." No one ever mentioned that happiness is hard work.

But the truth is, after we've fallen into each other's arms and declared our mutual passion, after we've gone still further and said "I do," that's when the real story begins. And that story is full of joy and tenderness—but it's also full of frustration and self-discipline.

By definition, marriage requires that two distinct entities become one. No matter how much in love we are, making two entirely separate individuals into a single unit is not an easy task. R. C. Sproul once said, "If you imagined your mother married to your father-in-law, and your father married to your mother-in-law, you'd have a good picture of the dynamics of marriage." I dearly love both my own parents and my in-laws, but that quote always makes me smile, for it creates an image in my mind of two preposterous unions. I don't smile nearly as wide, though, when Sproul's point becomes plain in my own marriage.

A peaceful union is hard to achieve, and oneness

is not something that happens overnight. The marriage ceremony does not magically erase the differences between husband and wife, nor does it cancel our selfish natures. Married harmony requires instead an acceptance that conflict is bound to occur; it also requires a commitment to ongoing reconciliation—for a lifetime.

When all is said and done, intimacy demands
that we face the pain of our shortcomings;
to come closer to each other, our egos have to soften.

HENRY JAMES BORYS

〉〉

I am not afraid of storms for
I am learning how to
sail my ship.

LOUISA MAY ALCOTT

29.

Expect to go through cycles in your marriage.

Our romantic fairy-tale image of marriage leads us to expect that once two people marry, they will be happy forevermore, end of story. So when we run into long stretches of boredom or unhappiness, we doubt our love. After all, according to the dictates of our culture, if we're not happy, then something is wrong.

These thoughts may nibble at the underside of even the strongest marriages, particularly during the early years, before experience gives us greater perspective. As the years go by, though, we learn that like the seasons, our love has cycles. Sometimes, our marriage may seem as cold and dead as January—but if we wait, if we're patient, spring always comes once more. After being married for nearly seventeen years, I'm always surprised—and delighted—when I find myself falling passionately in love with my husband all over again.

It might have been easier to run away the first time November's chilly gray skies settled over my marriage. But just think of all the warm, sweet Junes I would have missed.

ROMANCE IN REAL LIFE

Each marriage will go through different seasons,
and each season will have distinct challenges
and specific blessings.
. . .No season lasts forever.
Our circumstances change and grow.

SUSAN ALEXANDER YATES

⸮⸮

Love is like a violin.
The music may stop now and then,
but the strings remain forever.

JUNE MASTERS BACHER

30.
Hold tight to hope.

The apostle Paul says that faith, hope, and love are the three things that last (1 Corinthians 13:13), and we talk a great deal about faith and love. We tend, however, to skim over hope, as though it were somehow not quite as practical as the other two, not essential to our daily lives. In reality, though, hope is immensely practical. It's the thing that carries us forward, even when our married love may seem dry and dead. Hope is the bridge that gets us over the dark times. It's what keeps us believing in the future, no matter what the present looks like.

The hope that Paul speaks of is not a cheery, optimistic attitude that somehow the best will always happen. Instead, the bridge of hope is anchored firmly on one side by our love and on the other by our faith in Christ; it spans the distance between the two. When we lack this sort of hope, we refuse to believe that God can change us—and we close the door to the future's possibilities.

In our marriages—as in the rest of our lives— our hope is the Lord. When we make room for His power to work in our lives, who knows what He will create?

ROMANCE IN REAL LIFE

No pessimist ever discovered the secrets of the stars,
or sailed to an uncharted land,
or opened a new heaven to the human spirit.

HELEN KELLER

၁ ၣ

May the God of hope fill you with all joy and
peace as you trust in him, so that you may overflow
with hope by the power of the Holy Spirit.

ROMANS 15:13

၁ ၣ

Our God is the God of the impossible.
He is the One who can bring about change
and growth in anyone.
We need not remain in the hopeless trap.
We must not give up on our mates
or on ourselves.

SUSAN ALEXANDER YATES

"Hope" is the thing with feathers
    That perches in the soul. . .
And sings the tune without words
    And never stops. . .at all.

EMILY DICKINSON

When you get into a tight place
and everything goes against you,
till it seems as though you could not
hang on a minute longer,
never give up then,
for that is just the place
and time that the tide will turn.

HARRIET BEECHER STOWE

31.

*Leave room in your relationship for both you
and your husband to grow and change.*

In many ways, I am not the same person I was when I got married. I have gained self-confidence and developed talents I was once afraid to explore. Becoming a mother changed me forever as well. And on the downside, I weigh about twenty pounds more than I did on the day I said "I do."

I am grateful my husband's love is flexible enough that he can give me room to grow and change. He too has changed over the years—but I find those changes only make him more exciting to me. I'm proud of the way he's grown.

I could hold onto the image I have of my husband and refuse to let it go. But in the end, that would kill our marriage's life. Instead, our love is a promise that holds true no matter what changes come—and within that promise's shelter, we each have room to stretch, to spread out, to grow into the people God wants us to be.

*Love is not love which alters
When it alteration finds.*

WILLIAM SHAKESPEARE

ROMANCE IN REAL LIFE

*One of the most powerful things
you can do to keep your heart open
is to be vigilantly aware of the images
you have about yourself
and your partner and let them go.*

EVELYN AND PAUL MOSCHETTA

{ }

Marriage for a lifetime demands both stability (that we hold ourselves faithful to the promises we have made) and change (that we recognize the changing context in which our promises are made).

EVELYN EATON WHITEHEAD
AND JAMES D. WHITEHEAD

32.

Build trust by expressing your feelings with both honesty and respect.

The only way my husband can understand me is if I let him know what I am feeling. This means I have to dare to be honest—and the truth can be difficult to face. What looks like honesty is often just dumping my feelings onto my husband's shoulders. It's far easier to blame him for my anxieties and disappointments, rather than face my own inadequacies and old festering wounds.

Respectful (and often painful) honesty demands that I form new habits. When I express my feelings to my husband, I need to listen for words that indicate I'm blaming him for my feelings. When I hear myself begin to blame—or when I sense the truth slipping away from me—I need to apologize, and then back up and begin again.

When a woman tells the truth
she is creating the possibility for
more truth around her.

ADRIENNE RICH

ROMANCE IN REAL LIFE

*Trust is telling the other person
who you really are and being willing to
share your most intimate thoughts and
feelings.
It's like handing your mate a jewelry box
full of precious stones. . . .*

KEVIN LEMAN

༈ ༈

Love is not love until love's vulnerable.

THEODORE ROETHKE

༈ ༈

The more you uphold the truth the more you
feel completely at ease in each other's company.
There is no pretense going on, no secrets kept,
no "seeming" to be one way while inside
thinking or feeling something else.
There is no controlling, manipulating,
or scheming to outsmart each other.

EVELYN AND PAUL MOSCHETTA

33.
*Practice listening with acceptance
and affirmation.*

(Rather than with a defensive or judgmental attitude.)

I want my husband to talk to me—but sometimes when he does, I don't like what he has to say. All too often, I have to confess I've responded with defensiveness or criticism. So it's no wonder he sometimes hesitates to share his feelings verbally. Why would he want to, when my reaction only plunges us into conflict?

If we want our husbands to trust us enough to talk openly and honestly, then we need to practice accepting what they have to say. We can deal with our own feelings of hurt or anger later, in another setting or at another time. But when our husbands take the risk of being verbally vulnerable, we need to affirm and accept what they have to say. Only then will they feel safe to share their hearts with us again.

*It is vitally important that we. . .
accept our spouse's emotions
without feeling threatened or being judgmental.*

KEVIN LEMAN

Learning to listen well
to each other
can be the most important
skill of our marriage.

EVELYN EATON WHITEHEAD
AND
JAMES D. WHITEHEAD

ROMANCE IN REAL LIFE

34.
Consider yourselves partners in all areas of your life.

(Spiritually, socially, financially, and emotionally.)

As husband and wife, our emotions do not always run parallel. I may be challenged and fulfilled by my job at the same time my husband is feeling stressed and drained by his work. My income may be increasing while he's worrying about his next raise. Or I may be deep in a spiritual depression, just when he is feeling spiritually excited and optimistic.

But if my husband is my partner, then I will not stand separate from him while he suffers—and vice versa. Together we bear each other's sorrows and share each other's joys.

If one of you is in emotional pain the other cannot be separate from it.
This means that when one of you is angry that the other can't simply dismiss it by saying, "It's your problem, deal with it."

EVELYN AND PAUL MOSCHETTA

Carry each other's burdens,
and in this way
you will fulfill
the law of Christ.

GALATIANS 6:2

35.
*Never assume you know all
there is to know about your husband.
Continue to enjoy marriage's ongoing discoveries.*

*(A lifetime is too short a period to learn
everything about another human being.)*

One reason some marriages fail is because partners are bored. Spouses assume they know everything there is to know about each other—and familiarity breeds both contempt and boredom.

In reality, though, we will never know everything there is to know about our husbands. We may see only our image of who they are, and assume we know all there is to know—and all the while we fail to perceive the amazing quirks and startling changes that hide behind the familiar faces.

If boredom has begun to creep into your marriage, you don't need a new spouse—but you may need new eyes. When you begin to open your heart to the person your husband really is (not the old, familiar image of him you've been holding onto), you may be surprised by what you see.

*The real voyage of discovery consists not
in seeking new landscapes but in having new eyes.*

MARCEL PROUST

36.
Laugh often and laugh together.

I can't imagine what marriage would be like if my husband and I couldn't laugh together. I've never known anyone else with whom I've laughed more. Many times, laughter defuses our tension when we're fighting. And I'd hate to be a single parent and have to bite back my laughter all alone, with no one whose eye I could catch when my children were being impossible. . .or silly. . .or wonderful.

Whether we're lying in bed in each other's arms or fighting about something ridiculous, in the end our shared sense of humor binds us tighter together.

We cannot really love anybody
with whom we never laugh.

AGNES REPPLIER

﹖﹖

Shared laughter is erotic too.

MARGE PIERCY

Each day, and the living of it,
has to be a conscious creation
in which discipline
and order are relieved
with some play
and pure foolishness.

MAY SARTON

CHAPTER TWO

*Relating as a Couple
with the Rest
of the World*

Marriage is a committed life together of love
for one another and creative involve-
ment in the world. . . .

EVELYN EATON WHITEHEAD
AND JAMES D. WHITEHEAD

37.

Don't expect your partner to meet all your social and emotional needs.

(Strive for a balanced life that includes your own friends, work, interests, and prayer life.)

A few years ago I confided to a friend what were some legitimate frustrations in my life; I was experiencing needs that just weren't being met. But when I began to blame my husband for my feelings of frustration and need, my friend told me this story:

Suppose, she said, you were out of milk and bread. Milk and bread are good things to have, things your family genuinely needs, so you go to the nearest store to get these items. The nearest store, though, happens to be a hardware store. You know it's a well-stocked store, filled with the finest hardware around, and you confidently enter the door, certain you'll be able to find what you need.

"I'd like some milk and bread," you say to the man behind the counter.

And of course he shakes his head, and says, "I can't give you any."

"But I need milk and bread," you insist. But no matter how you plead with him, even if you cry, even if you get so angry that you shout and threaten to never come in that store again, he still won't give you the milk and bread you need. He can't; he doesn't have any in his store.

That's what we're like, my friend continued, when we try to force our husbands to meet our every need. They can't. No matter how many wonderful things they can offer us, they don't have everything we need. Getting hurt and frustrated accomplishes nothing. We have to take some of our needs somewhere else.

God doesn't want me to find my total fulfillment in my marriage. Instead, He meets my needs not only through my husband but also through my friends, my work, and my private relationship with Him.

The human heart wants an infinite love.
If the marriage partners seek this in each other
they are bound to be disappointed and frustrated.

M. Basil Pennington

38.
When needed,
seek professional help for your marriage.

(No book—not a book like this or any other
of the excellent self-help books out there,
nor the weightier professional tomes you can easily
find—is a substitute for professional counsel if you're
having a serious problem with your mate.)

When our bodies are sick, we go see a professional (although some of us put it off longer than we should). We understand, though, that our physical health is a priority; we cannot function well in any area of our lives when we are sick. When our own efforts to care for our bodies fail, then we seek the help of a doctor, someone who knows more than we do, someone trained in the healing profession.

But when our relationships with our husbands are seriously ailing, we often resist seeking professional help. We may complain about the symptoms to our friends, but complaining seldom brings healing. While professional counselors have no pills to magically cure our marriages, they can offer us concrete, practical strategies to begin the healing process.

Let's value our marriages enough to take care of them by whatever means we can—including, when necessary, seeking professional counsel.

ROMANCE IN REAL LIFE

Love will find its way
Thro' paths where wolves would fear to prey.

GEORGE GORDON, LORD BYRON

Psychologist John Gottman, author of *Why Marriages Succeed or Fail,* identifies the following serious warning signs, which he calls the "The Four Horsemen of the Apocalypse":

Criticism
Contempt
Defensiveness
Stonewalling

If you're interested in a serious but readable book on what makes marriages work and what makes them fail, take a look at Gottman's book.

ROMANCE IN REAL LIFE

39.
*If you can,
look to the strengths of your parents'
marriage—and practice those qualities.*

*(Or, if this isn't part of your heritage,
find an older couple in your church
or community to use as role models.
Don't miss opportunities to thank
them for their legacy.)*

When I was growing up, my parents' love for each other was one of the givens in my life. I saw them holding hands and kissing; I heard their whispered I-love-yous. I knew that two people could still be deeply in love after years of marriage.

When I'd been married a few years, my husband and I hit a long, dry patch when our love seemed to grow tired and resigned. Some friends told me this was normal. "After all," they said, "the honeymoon's over." But I refused to believe it.

I had watched my parents' marriage for too long to accept that my own marriage was destined to be dry and hopeless forever. I took hope from my parents' relationship, and I worked hard and stubbornly to move my marriage forward to a still deeper love and joy. Today, I find I continue to fall in love with my husband year after year, just as my parents do as well.

ROMANCE IN REAL LIFE

Each long-married couple will likely have a different lesson to teach. Whatever it is, we can learn and take hope from these experienced husbands and wives.

*A successful marriage is not a gift;
it is an achievement.*

ANN LANDERS

40.
Allow outside friends to enrich your marriage.

*(Everybody needs at least one second-best friend [your
mate should be your best friend],
someone who will just care, not offer solutions to your
problems. Like the suggestions in this book, a lot of
solutions are, at least on one level, commonsense—
and yet they are hard to execute in real life.
Often we don't need someone telling us
what we already know.
What we do need is someone who will love us even
when we are trying out solutions
that make no sense to anyone else.
If I were special-ordering this person,
this person would be as mum as
a priest in the confessional.)*

By this point in our marriage, my husband has
learned that my closest friends are one of our relationship's assets. He's aware that regular talks with
my truest friends help keep me balanced and happy,
which only adds to the health of our marriage. In
fact, when I'm being particularly emotional and
unreasonable, he's been known to suggest, "Don't
you want to give Tammy a call. . .or Patty. . .or
Faith?" He knows that spending time talking with
one of my friends will help me return to our own

relationship with a better sense of perspective, feeling less insecure and defensive. And talking with my friends definitely improves my sense of humor.

I've had women friends, though, who simply enjoyed husband bashing. No matter what I told them, they always fanned the flames of conflict between my husband and me. These friends were no asset to my marriage.

A true friend helps you to see the truth—and loves you no matter what.

Therefore encourage one another
and build each other up.

1 THESSALONIANS 5:11

⸮⸮

Two are better than one. . . .
If one falls down,
his friend can help him up.

ECCLESIASTES 4:9–10

41.
Don't turn to a male friend as a confidant.

(Especially if he is of your own generation.
The road to an unintended and
destructive intimate relationship
is paved with good intentions. . . .)

I'd never do that.

Don't be silly; that could never happen to me.

We're just friends. We both have too many morals to do anything wrong.

The thing is, though, moral people, Christian people, sometimes end up in trouble. Most of them didn't set out to commit adultery. But they allowed themselves to be in a situation where little by little they became close to someone other than their spouse. All marriages go through occasional times when one or both partners don't feel their needs are being met; during these times we're particularly vulnerable to forming a relationship with someone who seems to offer what we're missing. But what starts out as friendship can gradually move toward romance and sexual intimacy.

If you don't want to cross that line, set your protective barrier well back. Don't expect your will-power to save you when you're standing with your toes on the line. None of us are that strong.

God wants marriage to be a mirror that reflects the unconditional love, security, and trust He offers us. Adultery shatters the mirror.

King Solomon's warning against adultery:

Drink water from your own cistern,
running water from your own well.
Should your springs overflow in the streets,
your streams of water in the public squares?
Let them be yours alone,
never to be shared with strangers.
May your fountain be blessed. . . .

PROVERBS 5:15–18

Being true to [my partner]
is the same thing as
being true to myself.

HENRY JAMES BORYS

42.

If you're unhappy with your mate, share this distress only with your counselor.

(A pastor, professional counselor, or a second-best friend may be your counselor—but not friends who don't meet the above requirements for circumspection. As much as we may like them, most people don't. Spreading your marriage troubles only ensures that after you and your mate make up, your friends will continue to dislike your husband.)

I'd hate if my husband got together with "the guys" to laugh about his "old lady's" foibles and complain about his "ball and chain." In fact, I'd be desperately hurt. I rely on his loyalty to me. I was married for a few years, though, before I realized that when I spent time with a group of women laughing and complaining about our men, I was no better than those insensitive, sexist husbands I despised.

Going to a counselor or a good friend for support and insight is very different from complaining about my husband to anyone who will listen. I don't talk about my friends behind their backs. So why would I betray my best friend—my husband?

Disregarding another person's faults preserves love.

PROVERBS 17:9 NLT

43.

*The most important lesson you can teach
your children is to respect their father.*

*(The only way you can do that is by example.
Go out of your way to show your children
how much you care about their dad.
If you open your mouth, let something complimentary
and supportive push criticism out of the way.)*

All too often I allow myself to express to my children my marital exasperation. I roll my eyes and sigh when my husband forgets some important item the family needs; I snap at him over supper; I complain about his inability to sort laundry. These are little things, granted—but I should be as loyal to my husband in front of my children as I am to the rest of the world.

*When we as partners are able to create harmony
between us, the whole family benefits.
Having parents who are in sync and connected
with each other in a loving way
gives children a sense of well-being
and makes them feel good about themselves.*

EVELYN AND PAUL MOSCHETTA

ROMANCE IN REAL LIFE

44.
Resolve to settle any disagreements over child management out of the kids' hearing.

This is tough practice to follow, especially when our kids sometimes seem omnipresent. However, when I allow my children to sense that my husband and I don't agree on a particular discipline issue, I confuse them. What's more, they seem to engage even more in whatever inappropriate behavior has been the source of tension, as though they're purposefully testing us.

When the problem is recurring and ongoing, I've found that my husband and I need to schedule an occasion when we can sit down and work through our differences. No matter how sharp our disagreement has been, usually all we need to find a resolution is commitment and some time alone.

The challenge in every marriage
is to recognize these differences,
to understand them,
and fit them together
so the couple can function as a team.

KEVIN LEMAN

♡ *There* are many good books on child rearing available. One excellent choice, a fat paperback by Stephen Garber, PhD, and two co-authors, is called *Good Behavior.* If you need some guidance on how to improve the behavior of a normal child with normal kinds of behavior and adjustment difficulties, this book often comes very close to giving the expensive advice you'd get in early sessions with a professional counselor. You can read just the first few chapters, and then refer as needed to subsequent chapters on managing specific problems. Other excellent works include those by Gerald Patterson, Lynn Clark, and others.

45.
*Remember that the family
you have formed with your husband
is now your primary relationship.*

*(Don't allow your parents or family of origin
to come between you and your husband.)*

Keeping this principle in mind can be difficult. After all, we've all been conditioned since birth to listen to what our parents want us to do.

But while we continue to honor our parents, we can no longer allow their influence to come first in our life. Instead, our marriages' health demands that we do what is best for our husbands, our relationships together, and the new families we have created.

*This explains why a man leaves his father
and mother and is joined to his wife,
and the two are united into one.*

GENESIS 2:24 NLT

*To be married is to have found
in a total stranger a. . .
true blood relative
even closer to us
than father or mother.*

MIKE MASON

CHAPTER THREE

*Strengthening Your
Marriage by Taking
Care of
Yourself*

Fidelity in marriage, the survival and
  growth of intimacy between us, is
  grounded in another kind of intimacy:
  my awareness and love of myself. . . .
  Self-intimacy—the virtue which allows
  me to love, care forand accept myself. . .
  is at once a virtue required for marriage
  and a virtue which is especially tested
  and developed in marriage.

EVELYN EATON WHITEHEAD AND JAMES D. WHITEHEAD

46.
*We all have an "inner child,"
but don't expect your partner
to be that child's parent.*

Your "inner child" is that needy part of you who cries out for attention, the hidden child-self that throws tantrums and blinks back tears of hurt. She is usually demanding and a bit irrational—but she may also be the part of you who loves to play, who delights in small joys.

When we get married we often expect our husbands to take on the job of nurturing that child. We want our husbands to make us happy and keep us safe—and then when they fail to do that perfectly, we throw on them all the frustrations and hurt we still carry with us from our childhoods.

The truth is, God often uses a good marriage to help heal the wounded child you may carry inside you—but ultimately, as an adult, you are the only one who can care for that child. No one can make you happy. You are responsible for your own well-being.

*You are not responsible for
what happened to you in the past,
but you are responsible for
what you do with your life now.
Do you have the courage and strength
to be the expert of your own life?
Do you have the courage
to be who you were meant to be?*

CATHRYN L. TAYLOR

47.
*Learn some self-soothing techniques and
practice them for a few minutes.*

(Use them as needed when you're feeling stressed.)

Our emotions don't need to control our behavior.
Practicing self-soothing techniques is one way we
can take care of ourselves, especially those "inner
children" we just mentioned. For instance, when
I'm feeling stressed, tired, and hormonal, my husband's support and comfort helps me—but it's not
his job to keep my inner child from giving in to a
tantrum. Relaxation techniques can help me take
on that responsibility successfully.

As we practice these techniques, they gradually
become habit—and our emotions need no longer
be the tyrants that rule our marriages.

*Let us therefore make every effort
to do what leads to peace.*

ROMANS 14:19

Buy a book or an instructional tape that teaches
simple meditation, visualization, and breathing

techniques. There are many variations on a few themes, but some common ones are:

The Quieting Reflex by C. F. Stroebel
The Relaxation Response by Herbert Benson
The Relaxation and Stress Reduction Workbook,
 by Martha Davis, PhD, Elizabeth Robbins
 Eshelman, MSW, and Matthew McKay, PhD

Many excellent self-help programs and books exist on this subject. If you want to read seriously on the subject, try one of the New Harbinger books with psychologist Matthew McKay as one of the authors.

Here's a simple breathing exercise you can use to soothe yourself:

Find a place where you can be alone for a few minutes. Take off your shoes, loosen anything tight around your waist, close your eyes, and concentrate on your breathing. Make your breathing deep, abdominal (deep enough to push your belly up as you inhale), slow, and steady. Each time you exhale, say a one-syllable, calming word to yourself. Concentrate on doing this for 15–20 minutes, letting anything else, including intruding thoughts or nearby noises, fall into the background.

48.
Exercise.

(Contentment in your relationship begins with contentment with yourself. You will feel better about life in general if you exercise regularly.)

When we're juggling our lives as fast as we can, we often drop the exercise "ball." After all, we reason, the world will not end if we fail to make time in our lives for exercise. We'd all like to be thinner, of course, and we may feel guilty we're not taking better care of our bodies—but our responsibility to exercise simply seems less pressing than all the other obligations in our lives.

In reality, though, we usually have our priorities mixed up. This realization recently came to me: If I fail to clean my house today, that failure will have little if any impact on the future ten years from now. But if I fail to exercise today, ten years from now I may be overweight, out of shape, and aging far more quickly than I need to be.

Regular exercise may seem to have little bearing on the rest of our lives. God created us, though, as beings made up of hearts, minds, and bodies. Exercise will make us feel better physically—and when we exercise, our spiritual lives, our intellectual lives, our relationships, and even our most intimate sex lives will be enhanced.

ROMANCE IN REAL LIFE

If I am [unhappy with who] I am, I am
not able easily to sustain a relationship. If
I must defend a fragile sense of self. . .
then flexibility and compromise will be
hard. In either case, it will be difficult
for me to come close to you. . . .

EVELYN EATON WHITEHEAD
AND JAMES D. WHITEHEAD

You don't have to be Suzanne Somers, sweat to the oldies with Richard Simmons, nor have an expensive and time-consuming gym-based routine with a personal trainer. Start with doing better than you already are (for example, walk for half an hour three times a week, if you're mostly sedentary now). Whatever you choose to do, you should make your heart beat faster without being so out of breath you can't speak. As a general principle, you should talk with your primary care doctor before you start any exercise program that is a significant departure from your routine. There are many excellent books on personal fitness activities, but none are a substitute for discussing your personal assets and liabilities with your doctor (though don't be surprised if she refers you to another source for additional information).

49.

Practice speaking positively.

*(When your partner—or anyone else—
asks you how you are, take a deep breath,
pause a few seconds, and silently
count your blessings before you speak.)*

Complaints come easily to our lips. But cultivating the habit Lee recommends here will not only make our interactions with our husbands more positive, it will also make our general outlook on life less negative. What's more, a grateful heart is a pleasure to others—including God.

*. . .Make music in your heart to the Lord,
always giving thanks to God
the Father for everything,
in the name of our Lord Jesus Christ.*

EPHESIANS 5:19–20

ROMANCE IN REAL LIFE

50.
*When it comes to anger,
ventilation is not a breath of fresh air.*

*(For many years therapists encouraged clients
to "ventilate" or "blow off steam"
by screaming, punching a pillow,
or expressing their feelings verbally.
Subsequent research suggests that
any brief benefit a person feels
after these activities is usually undone
by the fact that these behaviors tend to
a) make a person angrier, and
b) solidify a person's sense of being wronged.)*

Practice letting go of your anger rather than holding on to it. You may want to visualize your anger as a tangible object you place in God's hands. Or practice a deep-breathing exercise, where you exhale your anger and inhale God's peace and forgiveness.

Remember, forgiveness is not a gift you magnanimously (or grudgingly) grant your husband. Instead, forgiveness will set your own heart free as much as it does your husband's.

Anger is a volatile emotion.
It can lead to inflexibility and insult;
it can escalate a small concern
into a bitter battle between us.
While anger is an expectable component of conflict,
it need not become the dynamic that drives us on,
beyond our control.

EVELYN EATON WHITEHEAD
AND JAMES D. WHITEHEAD

﹔﹖

Forgiveness is not something we push ourselves
   to do for others,
      and it is not a pardon we grudgingly grant.
Forgiveness is. . .freeing ourselves from the
      burden of anger. . . .
Forgiveness is the healing flame that burns
      away the poisons.

EVELYN AND PAUL MOSCHETTA

51.

Always look for a silver lining, and lighten up.

*(Most of our problems are trivial
compared to the real problems of those
who are hurting around us.)*

Sometimes when we are juggling our lives frantically, trying desperately to keep everything smoothly up in the air, we become so focused on our own spinning lives that we lose our sense of perspective. The "balls" seem to come at us so relentlessly, we begin to feel as though we're trying to keep a set of bowling balls—or cannonballs—up in the air. And we suspect the world might end if one were to slip out of our grasp and crash to the floor.

Times like that, we need to take a break from our juggling routine and look around. When we do, we usually see how truly blessed we are. Others are struggling with burdens far heavier than our own. We may even realize that what we mistook for cannonballs are actually merely Ping-Pong balls!

The word "juggle" comes from the Latin word for "jest" or "joke." As adults, weighed down by countless responsibilities, we have often forgotten the sense of play we had as children. But if you watch a child playing, you'll see how totally focused she is on what she's doing—and yet how free she is of self-consciousness and fear of failure. When we begin to "play" our juggling game, we may be surprised how even the busiest weeks are filled with joy. If we drop a ball now and then, the world truly will not end; in fact, since we do not play this game alone, we can even laugh, knowing that the divine Juggler will catch any balls we miss. Rather than seeing each responsibility and role as a heavy task, we'll find ourselves enjoying each thing we juggle a bit more. And our renewed sense of peace and pleasure will spill over into our marriage as well.

*The action of those whose lives are given to the Spirit
has in it something of the leisure of Eternity;
and because of this,
they achieve far more than those whose lives
are enslaved by the rush and hurry. . .of the world.
In the spiritual life it is very important
to get our timing right.
Otherwise we tend to forget that God. . .
is greater than the job.*

EVELYN UNDERHILL

52.

Make a regular time in your life for solitude.

As close as we may be to our husbands, we all need to spend time alone. In solitude we have a chance to renew our sense of perspective, our sense of who we are as individuals, and most of all our sense of God's presence in our lives. When we are alone, we refuel our hearts emotionally and spiritually; if we fail to make time regularly for this, we will soon find ourselves running on empty.

Even Jesus, God's Son, needed to get away from His disciples and followers now and then. The busier we are, the more desperately we need these quiet moments alone with God. We will have nothing to bring to our marriages if we do not take care of our own souls.

The nurse of full-grown souls is solitude.

JAMES RUSSELL LOWELL

Marriage is a solitary journey as much as it is a journey of two together.

After all, the first step to connect with each other must be to connect with ourselves. Otherwise, what is the meaning of intimacy?

HENRY JAMES BORYS

≀ ≀

*You will find that deep place of silence
right in your room,
your garden or even your bathtub.*

ELIZABETH KUBLER-ROSS

≀ ≀

*True silence is the rest of the mind;
it is to the spirit what sleep is to the body,
nourishment and refreshment.*

WILLIAM PENN

53.
Practice patience.

When I first began using a computer for writing, I was amazed by how much faster it was than a type-writer—but now, that little computer I had fifteen years ago seems archaic and slow. And in another fifteen years—or even two—the computer I'm using right now will seem just as dated and ponderous, because even as I write, computer companies are working to develop faster and faster machines.

We do not live in a patient world. All around us are fast foods, instant products, devices that will enable us to zip through our lives more quickly. We hate to wait. We want results—and we want them now.

But we will be frustrated and disappointed if we bring those expectations to our marriages. Most times, relationships grow slowly, almost impercepti-bly, the way a tree grows.

The Bible is full of the word "wait." Waiting means we stand with our hearts ready and open for God's blessing. We focus on Him, knowing that in His time we will see His hand at work. This is what patience is all about.

We believe and expect that we can have it all NOW.

We are in a rush to live life to the fullest and are fearful of missing out.

We desperately need to learn to wait.

SUSAN ALEXANDER YATES

૨૨

Patient endurance is what you need now,
so you will continue to do God's will.
Then you will receive all that he has promised.

HEBREWS 10:36 NLT

૨૨

If you are patient in one moment of anger,
you will avoid a hundred days of sorrow.

TIBETAN PROVERB

54.
Be willing to change.

Change is frightening. It asks us to go into an un-known land where we have never ventured before. We may not like everything about the people we are right now—but at least we're familiar with them. We know what to expect.

But God wants to transform us into His image. He wants to make us into our true selves, the people He created us to be—and again and again, He uses our marriages to tug us forward.

Like the caterpillar who is transformed into a butterfly, we cannot fly unless we let go of who we used to be.

> *To hoard—not only physical possessions*
> *but even past parts of myself—*
> *is to encumber myself on the journey.*

EVELYN EATON WHITEHEAD AND JAMES D. WHITEHEAD

≀≀

Do not conform any longer to the pattern
of this world, but be transformed. . . .

ROMANS 12:2

CHAPTER FOUR

*Resolving
Conflicts*

The conflicts of marriage penetrate to the heart—
right where they must deepen us.

HENRY JAMES BORYS

55.
Don't be afraid of conflict.

For whatever reason, most of us don't like conflict. We fear that conflict means there is something wrong with our relationship. It worries us. And we hate to have people upset with us. So unless we're stressed or exhausted or hormonal, many of us avoid conflict at all costs. We push our resentment and hurt beneath the surface, and we work hard to keep our marriages running smoothly.

But sometimes conflict is necessary. Conflict can clear the air between two people. It can make room for us each to grow. It can even bring us closer. When we trust our marriages and our husbands enough, we can risk anger and arguments, knowing that our love is big enough and strong enough to hold firm despite the storms.

Women are conditioned to be the peacemakers,
even at the expense of their true selves. . . .
Like the avoidance of quiet and solitude,
avoiding conflict keeps us
from reaching our full humanity,
our desperation and brokenness,
as well as our creativity and inspiration.

EILEEN FLANAGAN

Willingness to accept conflict as inevitable and even as potentially valuable need not mean that we find it pleasant to be at odds. But it does mean that we are willing to acknowledge and even tolerate this discomfort that our conflict brings, in view of the valuable information it provides about our relationship and ourselves.

EVELYN EATON WHITEHEAD
AND JAMES D. WHITEHEAD

Flowers grow out of dark moments.

CORITA KENT

The idea that conflict is healthy
may sound like a cruel joke
if you're feeling overwhelmed by
the negativity in your relationship.
But in a sense,
a marriage lives and dies
by what you might loosely
call its arguments,
by how well disagreements
and grievances are aired.
The key is how you argue—
whether your style escalates tension
or leads to a feeling of resolution.

JOHN GOTTMAN

ROMANCE IN REAL LIFE

56.
Learn to express your anger constructively.

(Read on for some specific techniques.)

Living as closely to another person as we do in marriage, we can't help but rub each other the wrong way. We each have prickly egos that clash against each other (until gradually, bit by bit, they are worn smooth). Although marital conflict is normal and even healthy, it also can be hurtful and destructive.

When we give in to our anger, most of us tend to wield it like a weapon against our husbands. We go for the throat, trying to do as much damage as we can. When we do, our conflicts are not constructive but the opposite.

Anger is a little like a spade, those sharp digging devices. A spade can be used as a deadly weapon—but it can also be used to turn the earth for a new garden. Inevitably, we will be at odds with our husbands from time to time—but we do not need to attack them with our anger. Instead, used properly, anger can be the tool that opens the soil of our marriages so fresh life can grow.

Anger is a vital valid, natural emotion.
As an emotion,
it is in itself neither right nor wrong.
The rightness or wrongness
depends on the way
it is released and exercised.

DAVID AUGSBURGER

57.

*Whatever your frustrations with your husband,
remember that you are the only one
you can change.*

If only he'd talk more. . .

If only he were more romantic. . .

If only he would share his feelings with me more often. . .

If he would just stop that irritating habit. . .

Most of us wives have a list we keep in the back of our heads, itemizing our husbands' irritating characteristics, the ones we'd most like to change. I know from experience that it's all too easy for me to focus on the ways I'd like my husband to be different.

Many of my frustrations are legitimate. And I know that some wives deal with husbands who have problems far more serious than the ones I put up with. But no matter how serious or legitimate my concerns, insisting that my husband change only creates resentment on his part and frustration on mine. I cannot force my husband (or anyone else) into the shape I'd like—even when I know that shape would be far more healthy. . .or spiritual. . .or conducive to family peace.

My husband's irritating qualities may never go away. Once I accept that, once I stop wasting all my energy on a lost cause, I can look at myself and see how I can behave differently instead. Ultimately, the only person I can change is myself.

I suspect it's a little like that kernel of wheat Jesus spoke of in the Gospels: Until the grain fell into the earth and "died," it could never grow and be fruitful. By the same token, when I allow myself to bend or even break, God's creative power is free to work, both in my life and in my marriage.

"I tell you the truth,
unless a kernel of wheat falls to the ground and dies,
it remains only a single seed.
But if it dies, it produces many seeds."

JOHN 12:24

⸮⸮

Every time I held out in an argument,
every time I wanted things my own way,
every time I wanted [my partner]
to change instead of me—
these were all perfect chances to die [to my ego].

HENRY JAMES BORYS

ROMANCE IN REAL LIFE

Everyone gets broken, at least a little, on the
wheel of love, and the breaking that takes
place is like nothing else under the sun. . . .
But in the case of those who hang on to
love. . .the ruin that occurs, the internal
debacle,is not in the place of love. . .
but rather in the palace of the ego. And
that makes all the difference in the world.
It is one thing to wreck the ego. But it is
quite another, and indeed the very opposite, to make shipwreck of the soul.

MIKE MASON

58.
Accept the people you are.

As husband and wife, we come to each other with a lifetime of history that formed us into the people we are today. No matter how much we love each other, neither of us will be able to erase the shape that heredity and environment have given us.

Instead, maybe we should simply accept that we are who we are. God was a part of the forces that influenced our identities—and if we commit our lives to Him, He will continue to work as He transforms us both into our true selves, the selves He created to glorify Him.

I find that all too easily I try to run ahead of God. But true trust and surrender to His will means I accept circumstances as they are right now—including myself, including my husband.

I am as my Creator made me,
and since He is satisfied, so am I.

Minnie Smith

A leading researcher in marital therapy recently concluded that helping unhappy couples change one or both partners' behaviors only goes so far. A large portion of relationship enhancement has to be about accepting our spouses with many of their shortcomings intact or only partially improved.

59.
Do something different.

(Whatever it is that you want to change in your relationship, believe me—doing more of the same thing that fails every time is a formula for failure. Don't wait for your husband to try a new approach; instead try doing one thing differently yourself.)

$\mathcal{S}ometimes$ my husband and I get in a rut. Week after week, month after month, sometimes even year after year, we go around the same self-defeating circle. We're locked in a power struggle, neither of us willing to give in and change. And then we end up having the same fights over and over. I sometimes think we might as well make a tape recording and then just push the play button every now and then; it would save us the effort of going through that same fight all over again.

As Lee just said a couple of pages ago, none of us are going to become totally different people overnight. It would be overwhelming (not to mention unrealistic) for me to think we could. Instead, I can choose to do just one concrete thing, even a seemingly minor thing, differently. It might be something as small as taking a deep breath and asking God for patience before we run through that same old fight again. Or it might even be saying "I love you"—or giving my husband a kiss—or just reaching for his hand—the next time he and I start to wear that rut a little deeper. Clinging to my resentment, waiting for my husband to make the first small move, is a waste of time when there's no need to wait: With God's help, I can make that first tiny leap toward the mature and loving relationship I want to have with my husband.

I discovered I always have choices and sometimes it's only a choice of attitude.

JUDITH M. KNOWLTON

In an intimate relationship, one person often must step out ahead—to free the relationship from old patterns, so that both can grow. Growing in a relationship is often like a game of leap-frog: one leaps while the other stands still. If we insist upon fairness, upon growing simultaneously, we will only wait for each other to take the first leap. Then neither of us moves.

HENRY JAMES BORYS

60.

*Don't try to solve a sticky problem
with your partner if you or he is overtired, ill,
or already upset about something else.*

Sometimes my need to talk things through now is really just my need to be in control. I find that things go much better if I'm patient and wait for the right opportunity, a moment when we can bring our full attention to the problem without the issue being complicated by tensions that really stem from another source. The world will not end if I wait until we're both rested and calm to address a particular conflict. After all, we have our whole lifetime to work on our relationship.

*Conflict always holds the choice between
creative and destructive responses.
The choice we make determines
the outcome.*

HENRY JAMES BORYS

61.
*Try hard not to
"let the sun go down on your anger."*

*(Grudge holding interferes with further
opportunities to enjoy and care for each other.)*

Lee may sound as though he's contradicting what he just said on the page before, but really he's not. Waiting for the right moment to deal with a problem is very different from nursing a grudge. We may have our entire lifetimes to work on our marriages—but at the same time, why should we miss a moment of joy, simply because we couldn't bring ourselves to let go of our hurt and anger?

*Cling to your grudges and you will
suffocate your marriage.
Take a chance on letting them go
and feel the freedom.*

KEVIN LEMAN

A fit of rage or a sulk has its secret attractions. Were that not so, most people would long since have acquired a little wisdom.

CARL JUNG

To be wroth with one we love
Doth work like madness in the brain.

SAMUEL COLERIDGE

Never go to bed mad. Stay up and fight.

PHYLLIS DILLER

62.
When you fight, avoid global labeling.

(For instance, "You're always selfish";
"You're such a jerk"; "You never listen";
"You're so stupid". This overheated,
"over inclusive" language has the effect
of making you plenty angry, since it convinces you
that your husband is totally despicable.
And it promotes no compromises.)

I have to confess that I'm guilty of this bad habit. In the midst of a fight with my husband, I find myself remembering all the other times he behaved in exactly the same irritating way. Suddenly, our marriage takes on an entirely different light; instead of seeing the man I truly adore, I perceive a selfish, thickheaded man who fails me again and again in the same frustrating ways.

But when I say to my husband, "You always. . ."; "You never. . ."—or when I sink still lower and express my anger with some juvenile insult, I accomplish nothing positive. Instead, he becomes understandably defensive, and our argument only escalates. The real issue becomes obscured by our building anger.

*Make no judgments
where you have no compassion.*

ANNE McCAFFREY

Lee's perspective:

If you and your husband are in the habit of using "over inclusive" language when you argue, agree on a penalty each time you catch yourselves. I recommend this technique: each time you catch yourselves, put an agreed-upon amount of money in a jar; hopefully you'll take a while to fill the jar, but when you do, send the money to charities.

63.
Use I-messages.

(Statements that begin with "I feel. . . ,"
"I think. . . ," "I want. . ."
to tell your partner how you're doing,
instead of You-messages, which blame,
inflame, and create division. Add
". . .when you. . ." to your I-message as needed.)

You make me so mad.
You never understand.
You hurt me.

Most of us use You-messages like these when we fight with our husbands. You-messages place the blame for our feelings squarely on our husbands' shoulders.

When we use I-messages, however, we take responsibility for our own feelings, while still communicating them to our husbands. Notice the difference:

I'm feeling grouchy today.
I feel as though you don't understand how
  important this is to me.
I feel hurt when you use that tone of voice.

At first, as we begin to use I-messages, we may feel

unnatural or artificial. But as we practice this technique, catching ourselves and rephrasing our words whenever You-messages creep back into our conversations, I-messages will become automatic. As we create a new habit, we'll find ourselves getting along better with our husbands.

Go to your bosom;
Knock there, and ask your heart what it doth know.

WILLIAM SHAKESPEARE

Here are some more examples of I-messages:

I worry when you don't call and come home late.

I'm upset when you spend money without talking to me about it.

I feel like you're not listening when you watch the TV while I'm talking to you.

I'm hurt when you forget our anniversary.

I miss you when you work so much.

64.

Take responsibility for your tone of voice.

*(Many things are communicated by your tone,
emphasis, and body language that add to,
subtract from, or distort your words.)*

Sometimes we don't fight fair. We communicate
our anger with our tone of voice, and then, when
our husbands react accordingly, we throw the blame
back at them. ("I don't know why you're getting so
upset," we say innocently, "I only said. . .")

We need to practice using our words to communicate our feelings constructively, rather than
pulling our husbands down with our voices and
body language. Try holding hands while you and
your husband discuss a sticky issue. You may find it
changes the tone of your discussion.

> *The tongue is a pen,
> which pressing deeply enough
> (and whether for good or for evil)
> will write upon the heart.*

MIKE MASON

Try this exercise: Read the following sentences, emphasizing a different word each time.

I never said you stole my money.

I *never* said you stole my money.

I never *said* you stole my money.

I never said *you* stole my money.

I never said you *stole* my money.

I never said you stole *my* money.

I never said you stole my *money.*

As you can see, although the words remain exactly the same, the meaning changes.

65.

Put this verse someplace where you can see it every day: "A soft answer turneth away wrath."

*(Sometimes there is no substitute for the
King James Version of the Bible, and
I think this isn't said better anywhere else.
Try making this verse your motto.)*

Sometimes I feel as though fights just happen to my husband and me; they overtake us out of the blue, spoiling an otherwise perfectly good day. But the fact of the matter is this: I have a choice as to whether I want a fight to happen or not. When I feel hurt or impatient, I can choose not to retort quickly with anger, and instead I can watch my tone of voice as I respond with a careful I-message.

This is the sort of verse I need to tape to my computer, post above my kitchen sink, and clip to the visor of my car. Maybe if I read the verse often enough, its words of reminder will stick in my head.

*Anger assures me that I am right
and [my partner] is wrong.
With anger, I do not have to face my own fault. . . .
Anger can be comforting,
if I am comfortable with not growing.*

HENRY JAMES BORYS

If alcohol figures regularly as a trigger for the stupid, hurtful things that come from your mouth, lower your level of alcohol intake. If you can't by yourself, get help.

66.

*If you and your mate have a persistent conflict,
add a new element to the situation.*

*(For example, when you recognize the same
old fight starting, agree to set a timer
and sit without saying anything for
ten minutes—or sing "Amazing Grace"
together—or have a thumb fight).*

I have to admit, my first response to this suggestion from Lee was, *Oh, come on. My husband and I would never do something that would seem so silly in the midst of a fight.* But then I stopped to think about it.

My husband and I have been having the same fight over and over the past few months: I think he's too hard on our oldest daughter; he thinks I'm too easy; and we go round and round the same old cycle of angry words. But if we agreed ahead of time to practice one of Lee's suggestions before we continued our argument, I suspect we'd end up laughing—and that would be a whole lot more fun than fighting. When we did return to our discussion, our attitudes would be far different, and our conversation would probably be more productive.

The course of true love never did run smooth.

WILLIAM SHAKESPEARE

67.

*To solve a problem,
look for a solution that worked for you before.*

When I glance back through my journals, I'm always surprised to find that throughout our marriage my husband and I have been discussing and resolving similar issues over and over. (For instance, I recently discovered that we argued over child rearing when we were the parents of toddlers, just as today we don't always agree on how to discipline our teenager.)

Even if you don't keep a journal, reflecting on the history of your marriage is a good practice. Past issues may be different from the ones you face today, but you'll likely find you can follow many of the same paths toward resolution.

What's more, looking back can give you a better sense of perspective. As married people, sometimes our conflicts seem overwhelming; we may be tempted to think we will never find our way back to peace. But we have worked through other conflicts in the past; we have lived through times of married stress and found our way back to loving harmony. When we once more find ourselves in the midst of marital conflict, we can take hope and wisdom from those past experiences.

*Whatever is has already been,
and what will be has been before.*

ECCLESIASTES 3:15

68.

*Never go out of your way
to prove your husband wrong.*

*(Unless there's a profoundly important reason to do so.
If your husband does or says something
that isn't life threatening—
or potentially embarrassing to him
if he does or says it elsewhere—
resist the temptation to let him know
you're right and he's wrong.)*

Oh, all right, I'll confess—I'm guilty of this. Until now, I'm not sure it ever occurred to me that no matter how certain I am that I'm right, I might choose to keep my mouth shut. After all, you'd think my husband would appreciate me sharing my greater wisdom with him, wouldn't you?

Thing is, though, he never seems to.

Marriage constantly challenges us to grow in humility. Isn't it amazing. . .and wonderful. . .and painful?

*For even as love crowns you so shall he crucify you.
Even as he is for your growth
so is he for your pruning.*
KAHLIL GIBRAN

69.

*Learn how to negotiate "win-win" solutions
and practice negotiating them respectfully.*

A win-win solution is one where both partners end up with something they want. One does not pay the price for the other's pleasure. Both are left with a good taste in their mouths. (For instance, recently, my husband and I were arguing over the time he spends at work when I want to him to be home with the kids so I can finish up my own work responsibilities. On that particular occasion, we reached this solution: On Monday and Wednesday he would come home early from work so I could work late, while on Tuesday and Thursday he got to come home as late as he needed and I would offer him no complaints. On Friday, we would both try to end our workdays early and do something fun as a family.)

Negotiating win-win solutions takes creativity and effort. But as wives, our resolve to find these answers reflects our commitment to the well-being of both ourselves and our husbands—and ultimately our marriage itself.

Love is a game that two can play and both win.

Eva Gabor

♡ *If* you can't figure out how to create your own win-win solutions, find a good self-help book or audiotape by someone with academic credentials (a licensed or certified therapist or professor at a reputable university), or find a live counselor with credentials and relevant clinical experience. Your personal physician isn't likely to be an expert, but she can usually refer you to one.

70.
Let go of the past.

In the midst of a fight, all too often I find the ghosts of old grievances rising back to life. My husband and I may start by fighting about his being a day late for my birthday—but before long, I'm reminding him of the time two years ago when he gave me an IOU for my birthday on which he never made good. . .and then the time seven years ago when he gave me nothing for my birthday except a too-small T-shirt. . .and the time when we were dating when he missed my birthday altogether. As I resurrect more and more old, bitter ghosts, my hurt and anger expand, while my husband's defensiveness grows. After all, in practical terms, what can he do to fix all those long-ago injuries?

Old ghosts have nothing to add to our marital conflicts. Leave them in their graves. Learn from the past and move on.

Memory is a good servant, but a bad master.

Nisargadatta

Individuals. . .can gnaw
on old grievances,
remembering them again
and again,
renewing them obsessively until
the shape of memory and desire
is permanently warped
along the lines of anger.

WILLIAM STAFFORD

71.

*No matter how unreasonable your mate is,
never attack his personality;
stick to the behavior you don't like.*

You are such an idiot!
You're a selfish pig!
You're a lazy slob!

Accusations like these can slip so easily from our lips. When they do, our words seldom change the behavior that angered us; instead, we only succeed in assaulting our husbands' identity.

I-messages that speak to the behavior, not the person, are far more effective—not to mention loving.

*Criticism speaks to the fault
with the person;
love speaks to the person behind the fault.*

HENRY JAMES BORYS

72.
Let some things slide.

*(It's okay to decide that some recurring arguments,
if they're not so poisonous they pervade every day,
can be shelved as unproductive.
You may privately think to yourself—
preferably with a fond shrug—
There he goes again. . . ,
but you can choose to be tolerant
rather than confrontational.)*

Anyone who took Psych 101 knows about Pavlov and his dogs. Whenever Pavlov gave his canine friends a piece of meat he also rang a bell. Pretty soon the dogs were salivating whenever they heard the bell ring.

Well, I have a similar reaction whenever my husband utters certain phrases—except in my case, I don't start to drool. Instead, my blood begins to boil, and I respond with sharp words that soon escalate into a full-blown fight. Predictably, we find ourselves locked in an argument that accomplishes nothing.

But I don't have to go there. Pavlov's bell really didn't have much to do with food—and my husband's words aren't really a personal attack. I can choose to let his words sail right past me. I don't have to respond.

ROMANCE IN REAL LIFE

When an argument has proved nonproductive
in the past, there's really no point in going down the
same old road all over again. Occasions like these
are when we need to simply accept our husbands as
they are. If God wants to change them, that's His
job. In the meantime, with His help we can choose
to not "rise to the bait."

*Don't have anything to do with foolish
and stupid arguments,
because you know they produce quarrels.*

2 TIMOTHY 2:23

*Let us therefore make every effort
to do what leads to peace. . . .*

ROMANS 14:19

73.
Don't lecture.

*(If you're prone to preaching,
and moralizing, maybe you have a call
to the ministry—but your talents are
probably not going to be helpful in your
most important and intimate relationship.
Try a brief and explicit statement of whatever problem you're having—and then stop talking.)*

Oh dear, Lee's suggestion here is another one that hits me square on the nose. Maybe it's because I love words so much—but I often find myself saying the same thing ten different ways, explaining and expounding for far longer than my husband cares to listen. Eventually, his eyes glaze over; I suspect at that point he's simply tuned me out.

Words can be powerful tools. But sometimes a single sentence is far more effective than an entire book.

*When words are many, sin is not absent,
but he who holds his tongue is wise.*

PROVERBS 10:19

*Some people talk simply
because they think sound is more
manageable than silence.*

MARGARET HALSEY

74.
*Accept the fact that you
can't read your husband's mind.*

*(Avoid saying things like,
"You're only doing this to make me feel bad";
"You think I'm stupid";
"You think I'm too fat.")*

When we're feeling particularly insecure or sensitive, we tend to ascribe motives to our husbands that may in truth be the furthest things from their minds. When we do this, we're once more dumping the blame for our own negative feelings onto our husbands' backs.

If you feel in need of reassurance, try using I-messages instead to express your anxieties. When you do, your husband's response will be less apt to be defensive and impatient—and you're more likely to get the affirmation you're seeking.

*Love and faithfulness
always breed confidence.*

FRANCES DE SALES

75.

Don't expect your husband to read your mind.

I'm afraid this is something I often do on my birthday. In my mind, I build up a rosy image of how I'd like my husband to express his love for me on the anniversary of my birth. I try to keep my expectations realistic (I'm not shooting for moonlight and roses and an original serenade), so I'm all the more disappointed when my birthday once again doesn't measure up to my hopes.

"But you never said you wanted that. . . ," my husband protests.

"If I have to tell you then it doesn't count," I respond.

The thing is, though, realistically, I can't expect my husband to read my mind. If there's something I really want him to do—whether on my birthday or any other time—then I need to let him know what that is. When I do, he's generally more than willing to make me happy.

And if instead I want the unprompted, spontaneous expression of his heart—well, then I'd better be satisfied with the orthopedic sandals he gave me this year for my birthday.

A wife is a spiky,
complex creature brought into
conjunction with another spiky,
complex creature.
For the rest of their lives they will
be working out how to fit
into the small world
of marriage without
damaging each other.

JIMMY MEACHER

76.

*If you're having a disagreement,
jump right past the blaming,
and suggest a solution.*

It really doesn't matter who did what. Sometimes, I'm so quick to perceive my husband as the enemy. And my own fragile ego demands that I convince him he was wrong and I was right.

But what do I really hope to accomplish? As husband and wife, we are partners—so our goals should be the same rather than in opposition. When I trust my husband enough to believe he wants what is best for our marriage and for us both, then I find it far easier to simply skip all the defensive posturing and move on to the make-up scene.

*In a successful marriage,
there is no such thing as one's own way.
There is only the way of both,
only the bumpy, dusty, difficult,
but always mutual path!*

PHYLLIS MCGINLEY

♡ *Don't* try to make up if you have a vein bulging in your forehead and your heart is hammering like a locomotive. Take a little while (perhaps longer) to calm down. Use a calming method you know from experience works for you— go for a walk, listen to music, spend some time in prayer. If you don't have a method for calming yourself, try one of the self-soothing techniques mentioned earlier in this book. Learn to take your pulse and take a time-out if your pulse is more than 10 percent above its resting rate. When your heart is racing and you're pumped with adrenaline, you're better equipped for a "knock-down-drag-out" than a rational discussion.

77.
Try to avoid defensiveness.

(You may start out being in the right—
but because of your self-righteous anger,
in the end you may find you're just as much
in the wrong as your partner.)

Sometimes when I listen to my children bickering, I hear the echoes of my own conflicts with my husband. We never seem to outgrow our tendency to defend our fragile egos at all costs. Like quarrelsome children who fear someone will take something away from them, we are quick to lash out in self-defense.

But this is not the way Christ would have us interact with others, and certainly not with our husbands. Whether we are in the right or in the wrong, He wants us to seek reconciliation. If we follow His example, we will knock down the defensive walls we have built between us.

Defensiveness is a self-perpetuating illusion. . .
that if I give up an illusion about myself
(that I am relatively flawless),then I will lose my
worthiness as a human being; I will become less. . . .
There is only one door out of this trap:
face my need to grow.

HENRY JAMES BORYS

78.
Be the first to admit you're wrong.

(Even if your husband has been at fault as well.
You can quote me on this:
"Two wrongs don't make a right!")

"*But* he hit me first!" That's the old argument we've all heard children use. As parents, we know enough to explain to our children that violence—whether physical or verbal—never justifies violence. And yet we fail to practice this same truth in our own lives. We feel quite comfortable responding harshly to our husbands' sharp words.

According to the world's logic, two wrongs often do make a right; the wisdom of Christ looks like foolishness in a dog-eat-dog culture where the strongest person wins. But that's why Christ came to earth: to show us another, better way—the way of love. If we're following this path, then we will be quick to admit to our husbands when we have been wrong—even if they have been at fault as well.

The next time we fight,
instead of trying to be right,
perhaps we should take on a bigger challenge:
see who can get vulnerable first.

HENRY JAMES BORYS

79.
Don't be afraid to apologize.

(Even when you're certain you are the innocent one.
After all, you've probably missed
a few apologies you owed along the way.
Ask yourself how important this issue
really is in the big picture of your shared
history of intimacy and kindnesses.
When you're tempted to make a defensive excuse,
instead, simply say you're sorry.
You can always talk about the reasons for
your feelings when the tension is less intense.)

Remember that old line from *Love Story*: "Love means never having to say you're sorry"? It's not true. The fact is, love means saying you're sorry over and over, twenty times a day if need be.

A sincere apology requires humility. It asks us to put the well-being of our marriage ahead of our pride and our need to be right. It's not easy—but it's well worth the sacrifice.

You should run a thousand miles from such expressions as:

"I was right."

"They had no reason for doing this to me."
"The one who did this to me was wrong."

*God deliver us from
this poor way of reasoning.*

TERESA OF AVILA

80.
Be quick to forgive.

Sometimes my anger is self-feeding; the more I rant and rave at my husband, the more some perverse little part of me enjoys what I'm doing. So when he responds by simply saying, "I'm sorry," I don't always want to hear him. I want to hold on to my feeling of self-righteous rage.

Clinging to my anger, though, only means I make our conflict last that much longer. Making up really is a whole lot more fun than fighting.

> *"How many times shall I forgive my*
> *[husband] when he sins against me?*
> *Up to seven times?" Jesus answered,*
> *"I tell you, not seven times,*
> *but seventy-seven times. . . .*
> *Forgive your [husband] from your heart."*

MATTHEW 18:21-22, 35 (MODIFIED)

*Forgiveness is the cornerstone of our faith
and the hope for revitalized relationships.*

SUSAN ALEXANDER YATES

⸮ ⸮

Forgiveness is basically a letting go.
It's the hardest thing in the world,
but it's also the simplest.
Just let go.

KEVIN LEMAN

⸮ ⸮

A happy marriage is the union of two good forgivers.

ROBERT QUILLEN

81.
Keep fights short.

*(Contract with your mate to keep
the discussions of your conflicts to no more
than fifteen to thirty minutes at a time.
Set a timer if need be.)*

I tend to see conflict as a spontaneous fire that bursts out unexpectedly in my marriage. Many of the discussions I have with my husband, however, are predictable and recurring. We do not have to be passive participants in these conflicts, letting them rule our lives. We can control conflict rather than allowing conflict control us.

This means we may look at these points of disagreement as though we were running a business. When a particular issue arises that needs to be discussed, we simply set a time to talk it over. The time limit will help keep us on task; if we know we only have another ten or fifteen minutes to express our point of view, we'll be less likely to move away from our agenda by bringing up old and irrelevant issues. And when our business meeting is over, we can move on to another, more pleasurable activity.

Joy is love exalted;
peace is love in repose;
long-suffering love is love enduring. . . .
faith is love on the battlefield;
meekness is love in school;
and temperance is love in training.

Dwight L. Moody

ROMANCE IN REAL LIFE

82.
*Agree to have certain arguments only
a certain times of day, with no exceptions.*

When I bring up certain topics at bedtime or as my husband is getting ready for work, I never accomplish anything. I find myself feeling frustrated and upset when I should be settling down to either sleep or my own workday. Over the years, I've realized it's just not worth wasting my emotional energy on a fight that will accomplish nothing.

Sometimes, with children in the house, it seems like there is no good time to discuss an issue with my husband. Times like that I need patience. The issue probably won't disappear while I wait for the weekend or a quiet evening—and if it does go away, then it didn't need to be discussed after all.

It all depends on what I really want. If I want to simply vent my anger, well, then almost any time of day will work for that. But if the whole purpose of marital conflict is to find resolution, then waiting for the right moment is well worth the effort.

*A successful marriage demands a divorce:
a divorce from your self-love.*

PAUL FROST

83.

Try to respond to a complaint with an attempt to solve the problem.

(Complaining about something else about your partner only throws gasoline on the fire.)

Have you ever done this? Your husband complains that you always leave the car's gas tank empty—and you respond with, "Well, you never pick up your dirty socks." You see his complaint as a personal attack, and you respond with your own ammunition. Very quickly your discussion escalates into a fight that has little to do with an empty gas tank.

Once again, we need to train ourselves to think differently about conflict. If the purpose of conflict is to bring us closer together, then we can do without all the defensive posturing, name-calling, and personal attacks. Instead, we can choose to skip the fight and jump right into the solution.

*Forgetting oneself is not a refinement of love.
It is a first condition of love.*

LEON JOSEPH SUENENS

CHAPTER FIVE

*Sexual
Intimacy*

Sexual relationship is a path,
   not a destination;
it is an expression of love and holiness,
   not a god in and of itself.

EILEEN FLANAGAN

Sex is sacred ground.

MIKE MASON

84.

*If you're disappointed in
the sexual side of your marriage, get help,
but it's okay to start with self-help (read on).*

*(Dr. Joy Brown, one of the better radio
talk show therapists, says if you've decided
that sex is no big deal, you're probably not
doing it right. I believe the old saying that says
sex is 10 percent of marriage when it's good
and 90 percent when it's bad.)*

Sexual intimacy is a way to express our love and closeness with our husbands physically. I often think it's a little like the sacramental view of communion—it's both the symbol of something important and yet in a way it's bigger than a symbol; it's almost the thing itself.

When married sex is healthy and happy, it tends to fall in the background of your marriage; it's simply the expression of the entirety of who you are together. But when sex is not working, for whatever reason, this failure can overshadow the rest of your relationship. If you and your husband are unable to express yourselves sexually to one another, it usually shows there's a problem between you somewhere else as well.

Sometimes we're all tempted to just accept

things the way they are, rather than hope for change and be disappointed. But sexual intimacy can be improved. We don't have to be shy to bring our sex lives to God in prayer. He can direct us to the help we need to grow and heal.

The man's mission in marriage is to
meet the needs of his wife,
and the wife's mission is to
meet the needs of her husband,
in sex as in every other aspect of life.

KEVIN LEMAN

⸮⸮

Erotic love, if it is love, has one premise.
That I love from the essence of my being—
  and experience the other person in the essence
  of his or her being.

ERIC FROMM

*To be naked with one another is a sort
of picture or symbolic demonstration
of perfect honesty, perfect trust,
perfect giving and commitment,
and if the heart is not naked
along with the body, then
the whole action becomes
a lie and a mockery.*

MIKE MASON

≀≀

*Has not the LORD made them one?
In flesh and spirit they are his.*

MALACHI 2:15

85.

*Make sure your bed is big enough
to accommodate the range of needs it serves.*

*(Your bed should be the most comfortable,
private, inviting place in your house—
the place where both of you fantasize
about going during the day.)*

After more than a decade of marriage (closer to two decades, in fact), the sheets and blankets we received as wedding gifts are beginning to look frayed and faded. I noticed recently that even our mattress (also a wedding gift) isn't as comfortable as it once was. But in a household budget that includes three sets of school clothes, spending money on our bed is hard to justify. After all, my husband and I are the only ones who see it.

On vacation this year, though, our bed was piled with pillows, while under the plump comforter were the smoothest, softest sheets—and I noticed how excited I was about going to bed. Just getting between the covers was an event, one I anticipated all day long. The atmosphere of pleasure and comfort created an atmosphere where intimacy could flourish.

ROMANCE IN REAL LIFE

One of the most fundamental
and important tasks that
has been entrusted to marriage
is the work of reclaiming
the body for the Lord,
of making pure and clean
and holy again that which has been
trampled in the mud of shame.

MIKE MASON

Lee's perspective:

I suggest as a minimum a queen-size bed. They seem to be "out" right now, but my preference is for the modern waveless waterbed (the one with hidden tubes of water in a traditional-looking mattress outside). Whatever you and your husband prefer, try considering it a necessity rather than a luxury. I recommend that you invest in comfortable and attractive bedding as well.

Also, keep your bed mainly for whispered endearments, snuggling, lovemaking, and sleeping. Books are also okay, especially if they're a shared experience, but try not to bring your work to your bed.

86.
Make time to just hold your partner.

*(Do this when there is explicitly no demand for
sexual activity. Your husband will send you
signals if he wants more, but sometimes it just feels
good to be cherished. Talk to your partner,
using I-messages, as needed, to get the
"snuggling time" you want as well.)*

Babies who are held often are more apt to be emotionally and physically healthy. As adults, we have not outgrown our need for the warmth of human arms. When husbands and wives hold each other, they nurture each other's hearts, while they shelter each other's bodies. The sense of security helps create a marriage relationship where sexual and emotional intimacy can flourish.

*If we decide not to have sex,
so long as we have connected more deeply,
we still will have made love.*

HENRY JAMES BORYS

87.
Don't be in a rush during lovemaking.

*(Married people can and should take time to enjoy
and pleasure each other. "Scheduling" a
morning encounter, or any other time that works
for you, may be the only way to
make time for sex sometimes.)*

Remember when you and your husband were dating, the feeling of butterflies, the nervous joy you used to feel before a big date? Making a date for sex with our husbands can be just as exciting.

Spontaneity can be thrilling. So can anticipation.

*To plan for sex need not mean to routinize it.
It is more likely to ensure that we
have time to be lovers—
time to prepare for making love,
so that we can be really present to each other;
time to love each other well,
responsive to the rhythms of our own
and each other's pleasure;
time to share the special security
and well-being that lingers after lovemaking.*

EVELYN EATON WHITEHEAD AND JAMES D. WHITEHEAD

88.
Try out new positions thoughtfully and gently.

(Real life is not the movies.)

God wants our married sexuality to be creative, playful, joyful. Being open to new ways to express our love can add excitement and tenderness to our sex lives. But that doesn't mean we need to set ourselves unrealistic standards or engage in sexual gymnastics.

Your sex life belongs to you and your husband—and no one else. The pleasure and comfort of you two are the only standards.

Forget about stimulating each other.
Stimulate love and have patience.
The rest follows naturally. . . .
Spiritual growth can be
an aphrodisiac too.

HENRY JAMES BORYS

89.

*Be sure to communicate in the bedroom
as well as in the other areas
of your married life.*

No matter how well we know each other, none of us are mind readers. If there's something we're not getting in the bedroom, if there's something that makes us uncomfortable, if there's something we love and wish would happen more often, or something we simply hate, then we need to be vulnerable enough to share our feelings gently, without criticism. The more often we communicate openly about sexual issues, the easier it will become.

*Sharing your feelings with your mate
is not a one-shot deal.
It's a continual process of unraveling
the mystery of the individual.*

KEVIN LEMAN

ROMANCE IN REAL LIFE

Marriage is living with glory.
It is living with an
embodied revelation. . . .
It is living with a mystery
that is fully visible,
with a flesh-and-blood person
who can be touched and held,
questioned and probed
and examined
and even made love to. . .
but who nevertheless
proves to be utterly
and impenetrably mysterious.

MIKE MASON

90.
Seek help from books and videos.

*(There are many good books on married
sexuality that can be helpful for couples
who wish to enhance their sexual intimacy.
Also, a number of reputable sex education videos,
narrated by therapists, have been created for couples.
These are not pornography, though they're also
not for everybody. [This is not your high school
biology teacher with a plaster model of the
reproductive tract.] They can suggest ways to
enhance a couple's sexual enjoyment, whether
you are newlyweds or older folks who a) don't know
as much as you let on or b) are coping with changes
in sexuality wrought by aging or illness.)*

Within the context of our marriage, I suspect
that anything that enhances our love is perfectly all
right with God. I'd say that books and videos like
these fall under the same category as specific sexual
techniques—they may add joy and excitement to our
married lives, and sometimes being open to new
ideas and experiences can help us to grow in unexpected ways. But if something makes us uncomfortable, then we need to say so honestly—and respect
our husbands' positions as well.

ROMANCE IN REAL LIFE

"Everything is permissible"
—but not everything is beneficial.
"Everything is permissible"
—but not everything is constructive.
Nobody should seek his own good,
but the good of others.
. . . Whatever you do,
do it all for the glory of God.

1 CORINTHIANS 10:23–24, 31

For books on sexuality, check out the self-help section of any bookstore. Choose authors and evaluate their credentials the same way you would a professional counselor. There are definitely some helpful books on the subject written by the clergy, but look for evidence that the writer is also an expert on improving relationships and human sexuality as well. If you can do it comfortably, browse the shelves with your husband (on a slow shopping day in the middle of the week, if you find you're uncomfortable doing so at first).

ROMANCE IN REAL LIFE

A picture can be worth a thousand words, and there are a number of tastefully photographed (or drawn), professionally written books full of answers to questions people may be too embarrassed to ask. Usually the illustrations, thankfully, leave some things to the imagination. Let the illustrations be a vehicle for enlarging your repertoire, satisfying your curiosity, filling your gaps in knowledge, decreasing any embarrassment you have around the subject, and showing your partner what you like. Avoid any book that seems to concentrate on "plumbing" and "mechanics" to the exclusion of relationship enhancement. A tender and satisfying married sexual relationship and a satisfying emotional relationship are inseparable in real life. (Everything a married couple does together outside their bedroom is "foreplay.")

Two video series that are readily available (from the major book clubs, on the Internet, and from your music/record club) include the "Better Sex Video Series" and "Ordinary Couples, Extraordinary Sex." They are, in places, explicit, and if either partner is opposed to viewing and talking about them privately, then this is an option you certainly need not feel obliged to try. Use the private sharing of intimate educational materials to get past any anxiety (or ignorance) you may have about sexual matters; they can also be used as a tool to talk about and show your partner what you like and what makes you uncomfortable. Don't feel obliged to do anything that doesn't please you both, no matter what.

91.

*Make a time, light a candle or two,
find some scented bath oil,
and take a long hot bath together.*

*(If it's a prelude to lovemaking, well, fine—
but remember you can't believe
everything you've seen in movies.
The real goal of taking a bath together
is simply to build emotional intimacy;
you don't need to engage in
any underwater gymnastics.)*

As we juggle the demands of our children, homes, and careers, we often make our sexuality "ball" as tiny and compact as we can. That way it will be more manageable and won't interfere as much with all those other spinning balls we're trying so desperately to keep up in the air. Sex may even become one more item to check off our long to-do lists as quickly as possible.

Sometimes, though, each of us needs to set all those other balls down for an hour or so, and enjoy the physical bodies God has given us. Sharing a bath with your husband is wonderful way to simply enjoy his body and your own.

In sex, as in most other aspects
of our marriage,
to be "mature" does not mean
to fit some general criterion
of performance
but to have a developing
(and, perhaps, changing)
sense of what is appropriate for us,
what works for us.

EVELYN EATON WHITEHEAD
AND JAMES D. WHITEHEAD

92.
Seek sexual counseling.

(The number of couples who live with sexual disappointments that could be improved with counseling is heartbreaking. If you and your husband are experiencing sexual difficulties, ask your doctor or clergyman for a referral to a counselor who is specially trained in sexual incompatibility issues.)

Asking for help is always difficult. It's particularly difficult when we need help in such an intimate and private area of our lives. We may even feel that if we admit we need help, we are admitting to failure. The blow to our self-image may be more than we can endure.

So instead, we often try to minimize the importance of our difficulty. "Sex isn't all that important," we may say. "After all, we're not teenagers. We have more important aspects to our relationship."

But God wants us to be whole in all areas of our lives. We don't have to settle for anything less.

Intimacy is a challenge of the heart;
whether we grow from that challenge
or create misery for each other depends
. . .upon our vulnerability.

HENRY JAMES BORYS

If you seek out a counselor for specific sexual issues, this person may have a variety of degrees, but he or she should have relevant certifications (for example, through the American Association of Sex Educators, Counselors and Therapists or the American Association of Marriage and Family Therapists, or licensure as clinical social workers or psychologists).

93.
Take care of your physical appearance.

*(Remember how careful you were about
your grooming, your hygiene, and your clothing when
you were dating. Do no less for your mate now.)*

Days when we're juggling desperately, merely taking a shower in the morning may seem like a major accomplishment. And after all, aren't our husbands supposed to love us unconditionally, no matter what we look like?

Well, yes, they are. But think how much more attracted you are to your husband when he takes pains with his appearance. Taking the time to look your best is a gift that's easy enough to give your husband, a way of honoring him and telling him how important he is to you. It has a side benefit as well: Looking your best will also make you feel "sexier," more open to physical intimacy.

*If couples would put half the effort into marriage
that they put into courtship,
they would be surprised how things
would brighten up.*

BILLY GRAHAM

94.
Don't expect your sex life to make up for problems in other areas of your married life.

No matter how great your love life may be, sex alone cannot sustain a marriage for long. Eventually, it too will collapse under the weight of unresolved conflict and hurt that pervades the rest of your married life.

The best way to maintain an exciting and intimate love life is to practice all the other chapters of this book, as well as this one.

Fireworks don't occur in a void.
They happen when we make an effort
to keep the other stuff—
stuff like communication and emotional intimacy
and conflict resolution—in good working order.

KAREN SCALF LINAMEN

᛫ ᛫

Improving sex in a relationship begins
by improving the relationship
during the rest of the day.

HENRY JAMES BORYS

CHAPTER FIVE

*Your Marriage
and God*

To be married in the Lord
is to be able to experience this power and
presence of God in our life together:
God's healing love, in your love for me;
God's mysterious call,
in the challenge of development
and change in our life together;
God's delight, in the joy we share in sex. . . .

EVELYN EATON WHITEHEAD
AND JAMES D. WHITEHEAD

95.
*Begin and end each day
by praying for your partner.*

I find that when I pray for my husband regularly, I am changed. Maybe it's just that prayer opens the door for God to come into our relationship—and when He does, He puts His creative hand on all the different parts of who my husband and I are together.

Sometimes I bring my hurt and resentment to God—and I find my marriage works far better when I dump those feelings on God's shoulders rather than on my husband's. I can be completely honest, and yet gradually, as I pray, I'll find my anger disappearing. I begin to see things from my husband's perspective as well as my own; I'm able to let go of at least some of my anger. When I do, I can recognize my husband's needs as well as my own.

Other times, I give God my worries and concerns for my husband. I hate knowing my husband is unhappy at work; I hurt for him whenever my in-laws face times of crisis; and I fret about his health. (I wish he could live forever, and the thought of losing him terrifies me.) Prayer allows me to release these fears into God's hands, knowing those hands are big enough to hold them all. When I do, I'm free to experience again the peace God wants me to have.

And many times I simply thank God for my husband. I find that the more often I practice this prayer of thankfulness, the more I find to appreciate about my husband. Prayer like this helps me focus on my marriage's joy and takes my eyes off my complaints.

A successful marriage is dependent on inviting God into the relationship.

MANACHEM MENDEL SCHNEERSON

It is impossible to reckon how much a husband owes a wife or a wife a husband.
It is an infinite debt,
it can be paid only in eternity.

GOETHE

96.

*As you pray for your husband,
reflect on what he needs from you.*

One way that prayer for my husband changes me is that it helps me to shift my focus from myself to him. Instead of obsessing on my own needs, I can begin to see his as well. Neither of us will ever be able to meet all of each other's needs, nor should we. But I can allow God to use my life to touch my husband.

After all, God reveals Himself through His Body on earth, human beings whose hands and smiles and feet and voices are surrendered to Him. We usually understand that God wants us to minister to a needy world—but we often forget that He wants to live in our most intimate relationships of all, our marriages.

God, show Your love to my husband through me.

*Marriage is a channel of grace,
a way of experiencing God's love.*

Eileen Flanagan

97.

Pray daily for light on your own shortcomings in your marriage, and for help to change them.

I'm usually all too aware of the ways my husband lets me down from time to time—but I fail to recognize the ways I've failed him as well. The more I direct my attention at his failures and foibles, however, the more lifeless our marriage begins to seem.

Self-centered resentment produces nothing but dead, dry weeds. But new life springs out of the fertile ground of humility. As I practice times of prayerful self-examination, I begin to see the stubborn weeds in my own heart that are hindering my marriage's growth.

Reveal to me, Lord, the areas where I'm at fault—and give me the strength to change.

*Marriage is that intimate relationship
which tugs and pulls at two egos
in order to create the fulfillment of each—
if only we can humble ourselves enough to cooperate.*

HENRY JAMES BORYS

98.

*If you can, find a church where you
can worship together with other couples
who are at your stage in life.*

(It's good for your kids too.)

God often ministers to us through His Body, the
church. Worshiping with other married folk helps
us know we are not alone; others face the same
problems and joys we do. Together, we can help
each other grow.

*Our marriage will grow as we come
gradually and more powerfully
into the presence of each other,
our God and our selves.*

EVELYN EATON WHITEHEAD
AND JAMES D. WHITEHEAD

99.
*Each and every day,
take time to thank God for at least
one thing you appreciate about your husband.*

(Express your appreciation to your husband as well.)

When I was young I used to like to read a fairy tale called "The Snow Queen." In the story, the devil has a mirror that reflects only what is weak and ugly and unlovable. When his mirror gets smashed into myriad tiny fragments, the broken glass scatters through the world, lodging in people's eyes, changing their vision of the world.

Sometimes, I feel as though I have a piece of the devil's mirror stuck in my eye. Instead of focusing on the positive things about my husband, I unconsciously choose to dwell on the negatives. When I look back at our marriage, I no longer see the long history of love and joy; instead, I see only a dreary series of hurt and disappointment.

But there's an antidote for the devil's mirror. A fresh infusion of a thankful spirit soon changes my outlook. All I have to do to avoid being infected again is to practice daily thanking God for specific things I appreciate about my husband. These things may be as small as the breadth of his shoulders or the way he smiles, as mundane as the way he takes out the garbage every Tuesday or runs our cars through the car wash regularly—or as important as the way he's always at my side in church on Sunday morning or the way he never fails to forgive me when I've been wrong. The more things I find for which to thank God, the more I fall in love all over again with my husband. And when I express my appreciation to my husband as well, the atmosphere in our home changes too. Defensiveness and angry hurt tend to evaporate in the sunshine of a thankful spirit.

We are going to build a strong marriage friendship only if we choose to cultivate a thankful spirit.

SUSAN ALEXANDER YATES

$$\wr\wr$$

The person who has stopped being thankful has fallen asleep in life.

ROBERT LOUIS STEVENSON

ROMANCE IN REAL LIFE

100.
Pray together.

My parents pray together out loud each and every night before they go to sleep. This time of verbal prayer knits them together in a special way. As in so much of our married lives, however, what works for one couple won't necessarily work for another. If your husband is not comfortable expressing himself verbally, odds are he's not going to be happy if you announce that you and he are going to begin daily prayer meetings.

But that doesn't mean you can't make prayer a part of your relationship. Saying grace before meals, worshiping together at church, letting your spouse know you're praying for him when he's anticipating a particularly hard work day, asking for his prayers when you're stressed and upset—these too are ways to build prayer into your married life. Mutual prayer can be as simple as holding hands and silently coming together into God's presence.

You don't need to make it long
and religious sounding,
but get used to greeting God as a couple.

KEVIN LEMAN

101.

*Allow your marriage to crack open the
selfish ego we all have inside us,
so that you can come closer to God.*

We all have walls we've erected around our hearts, walls that are designed to protect our rights, our individuality, and our interests. These walls may seem like a necessity in the world in which we live, but the thing about walls is this: They not only protect us; they also keep people—and God—out.

As we live closely with another human being, learning to respect and love him as much as we do ourselves, at first we may find a brick here and there comes crashing down from our carefully built walls. Then whole sections wobble and fall. And eventually, as the years go by, like the walls of Jericho, the whole structure comes "a-tumbling down." Married life by its very nature demands that those high selfish walls fall flat. The process is uncomfortable, painful, terrifying. But it's the only way we can truly love and be loved.

And when the walls are down, when our hearts are naked and exposed, God too is free to come into our hearts in a new and intimate way.

Perfect love drives out fear.

1 John 4:18

ROMANCE IN REAL LIFE

I view my marriage as a spiritual path,
a way of life that expands and fulfills me,
that teaches me about myself and others,
that brings me closer to God.
This growth is usually not glamorous.
It is the ordinary things that teach the most:
deciding who changes the next diaper
or who gets the last bagel,
knowing when to speak and when to listen,
learning to give myself without giving up myself.

EILEEN FLANAGAN

The selfish self needs:

- To be right.
- To be perfect.
- To win.
- To be in control.
- To be pampered.
- Material things.
- More of everything.

ROMANCE IN REAL LIFE

Spiritual intimacy means consciously
using your marriage,
the everyday give and take between you,
and especially the difficult moments
as opportunities to rise above your ego
and express your best self, your spiritual self.

EVELYN AND PAUL MOSCHETTA

≀≀

That is what love does: it brings people out
into the light, no matter how painful that transition
might prove to be. Love aims at revelation,
at a clarifying and defining of our true natures.
It is a sort of sharpening process,
a paring away of dull and lifeless exteriors
so that the keen new edge of a person's true self
can begin to flash and gleam in the light of day.

MIKE MASON

≀≀

As iron sharpens iron,
    so one [person] sharpens another.

PROVERBS 27:17 (MODIFIED)